Critical Acclaim for
"How to Write a Winning Scholarship Essay"
By Gen and Kelly Tanabe

"This how-to book is full of good advice for college-bound students. Thirty essays with brief introductory notes give teens concrete examples of what works. Twelve essays that 'bombed' are also analyzed, pointing out pitfalls to avoid. Examples of interview questions and answers are also included. An excellent guide for all students who are hoping to continue their education."

–School Library Journal

"A wealth of tips, tricks, techniques, advice and useful strategies… absolute 'must-read' for anyone interested in competing for scholarship funds."

–Bookwatch, Midwest Book Review

"Sound advice for the college bound and useful for counselors as well as for libraries."

–Paula Rohrlick, KLIATT

"Thank you for writing your book. It really helped me to prepare for the interview. I had no idea what a scholarship interview would be like until I read the sample questions in your book. [The questions] helped me to prepare, and I learned a lot about myself. If it weren't for your advice, I would not have received this scholarship. Thank you!"

–Amanda Currie, Recipient of Goodnight Scholars Program

NO LONGER PROPERTY OF
SEATTLE PUBLIC LIBRARY

D0051161

Praise for Other Books by Gen and Kelly Tanabe

"Upbeat, well-organized and engaging, this comprehensive tool is an exceptional investment for the college-bound."

—Publishers Weekly

"Upbeat tone and clear, practical advice."

—Book News

"What's even better than all the top-notch tips is that the book is written in a cool, conversational way."

—College Bound Magazine

"Invaluable information ranging from the elimination of admission myths to successfully tapping into scholarship funds."

—Leonard Banks, The Journal Press

"A present for anxious parents."

—Mary Kaye Ritz, The Honolulu Advertiser

"When you consider the costs of a four-year college or university education nowadays, think about forking out (the price) for this little gem written and produced by two who know."

—Don Denevi, Palo Alto Daily News

"The Tanabes literally wrote the book on the topic."

—Bull & Bear Financial Report

"Filled with student-tested strategies."

—Pam Costa, Santa Clara Vision

"The first book to feature the strategies and stories of real students."

—New Jersey Spectator Leader

HOW TO WRITE A WINNING SCHOLARSHIP ESSAY

INCLUDING 30 ESSAYS THAT WON OVER $3 MILLION IN SCHOLARSHIPS

You can win or lose a scholarship with your essay. Learn how to write an essay that wins.

Step-by-step instructions on how to craft a winning scholarship essay and ace the interview.

Get valuable advice from actual scholarship judges and winners.

This book is a 'must have' for high school and college students who want to learn how to win scholarships.

Gen and Kelly Tanabe

Harvard graduates and award-winning authors of
The Ultimate Scholarship Book ▪ *Get Free Cash for College*
1001 Ways to Pay for College

Special contributions by Gregory James Yee

How to Write a Winning Scholarship Essay
By Gen and Kelly Tanabe

Published by SuperCollege, LLC
2713 Newlands Avenue | Belmont, CA 94002
650-618-2221 | www.supercollege.com

Copyright © 2018 by Gen and Kelly Tanabe
Previous editions: Copyright © 2016, 2014, 2012, 2009, 2006, 2002 under the title:
Money-Winning Scholarship Essays and Interviews

All rights reserved. No part of this book may be reproduced, stored in a retrieval system or transmitted, in any form or by any means, electronic, mechanical, photocopying, recording or otherwise, without the written permission of SuperCollege. This book is protected under International and Pan-American Copyright Conventions.

Credits: Cover design by TLC Graphics, www.TLCGraphics.com. Design: Monica Thomas. Cover photograph © iStockphoto.com/Gregobagel. All essays in this book are used with the permission of their authors.

Trademarks: All brand names, product names and services used in this book are trademarks, registered trademarks or tradenames of their respective holders. SuperCollege is not associated with any college, university, product or vendor.

Disclaimers: The authors and publisher have used their best efforts in preparing this book. It is intended to provide helpful and informative material on the subject matter. Some narratives and names have been modified for illustrative purposes. SuperCollege and the authors make no representations or warranties with respect to the accuracy or completeness of the contents of the book and specifically disclaim any implied warranties or merchantability or fitness for a particular purpose. There are no warranties which extend beyond the descriptions contained in this paragraph. The accuracy and completeness of the information provided herein and the opinions stated herein are not guaranteed or warranted to produce any particular results. SuperCollege and the authors specifically disclaim any responsibility for any liability, loss or risk, personal or otherwise, which is incurred as a consequence, directly or indirectly, of the use and application of any of the contents of this book.

ISBN13: 978-1-61760-132-3

Manufactured in the United States of America
10 9 8 7 6 5 4 3 2 1

Library of Congress Cataloging-in-Publication Data
Names: Tanabe, Gen S., author. | Tanabe, Kelly Y., author.
Title: How to write a winning scholarship essay : 30 essays that won over $30
   million in scholarships / by Gen and Kelly Tanabe.
Description: Belmont, CA : SuperCollege, LLC, [2018]
Identifiers: LCCN 2017053163 (print) | LCCN 2018000381 (ebook) | ISBN
   9781617601460 | ISBN 9781617601323 (alk. paper)
Subjects: LCSH: Scholarships. | College applications--United States. |
   Universities and colleges--United States--Admission. | Exposition
   (Rhetoric)
Classification: LCC LB2338 (ebook) | LCC LB2338 .T363 2018 (print) | DDC
   378.3/4--dc23
LC record available at https://lccn.loc.gov/2017053163

CONTENTS AT A GLANCE

TABLE OF CONTENTS

SPECIAL FEATURES

Stories & Advice from Winners & Judges

These stories of success and failure from students and advice from judges and experts are both entertaining and enlightening.

Judges' Roundtable: Chapters 3 - 7 - 10

We sat down with judges and experts from around the country to find out what it takes to win a scholarship. Read their frank advice on what students have done right and wrong.

This book would not have been possible without the selfless contributions of scholarship winners, judges and experts. They gave their time and shared their knowledge for your benefit.

We would like to recognize the special contributions made by Gregory James Yee.

We dedicate this book to all of the people who helped to make it possible. And to you, our dear reader, we hope you will use these lessons to create your own winning scholarship essays.

CHAPTER ONE

THE SECRET TO WINNING A SCHOLARSHIP

In this chapter:

■ Why you are 60 seconds away from the trash bin

■ How your essay or interview will make or break your chances of winning a scholarship

■ Why you can win even without straight A's

■ Who we are and why we know so much about winning scholarships

You Are 60 Seconds Away from the Trash Bin

If you witnessed the judging of a scholarship competition, you'd be surprised at how quickly decisions are made. It's not unusual for scholarship judges to decide in less than 60 seconds whether your application advances to the next round or gets tossed into the rejection pile.

With so little time, how do you capture the attention of these discriminating judges and improve your chances of winning? For most competitions the secret is in your **essay** or **interview**. These give the judges the insight they need to separate the winners from the runners-up.

If you are like the majority of scholarship applicants, you probably aren't sure what makes an essay or interview a "winner." And how would you know? It's unlikely that you have access to dozens of past scholarship winners who can share their experiences and show you their winning essays and interview answers. And it is even more unlikely that you've had the opportunity to speak with actual scholarship judges who can tell you exactly what qualities cause a candidate to stand out as a winner.

Obviously, anyone with this kind of access and knowledge has a tremendous advantage for winning a scholarship.

Now you can have this advantage.

In this book you will learn about scholarship winners, read their essays and interviews and learn the strategies that they have used to win more than $3 million in awards. (That amount is not a misprint. In fact, one incredible student received over $250,000 in scholarship offers!) You will also have the opportunity to hear from scholarship judges who will take you inside the selection process to reveal what they look for when choosing winners.

Unlike any other book on scholarships, by reading *How to Write a Winning Scholarship Essay* you will learn how to:

Find the scholarships you are most likely to win. We identify the best places to find awards and strategies for selecting those that you have the best chances of winning.

Craft a winning scholarship essay. The best way to learn how to win scholarships is from the experiences of others. You will read 30 actual scholarship essays that were used by students like you to win free money for college. Our complete essay-writing workshop will also guide you step-by-step through selecting a topic, writing about it and editing your own winning scholarship essay.

Avoid costly essay mistakes. Failure can be a great teacher, too. Through 12 essays that were less than exemplary (in other words they bombed), you will see exactly how to avoid the mistakes that have doomed others.

Interview confidently and skillfully. With comprehensive interview strategies and examples of over 20 questions you are likely to be asked along with successful answers, you will have everything you need to ace the scholarship interview.

Discover what scholarship judges want. Three special chapters called *The Judges' Roundtables* reveal what scholarship judges seek in selecting winners. This knowledgeable group of experts has seen thousands of applications and decided the fate of many applicants. Their lessons and advice are indispensable.

While the thought of making a winning impression in 60 seconds is certainly daunting, it is also an opportunity. By investing the time to learn the skills presented in this book, you will give yourself a tremendous advantage over other applicants. While most of them will be quickly eliminated within the first 60 seconds, your application will steadily progress through each round and ultimately help you to emerge from the competition a winner.

The Scholarship Strategies You'll Learn

This book is jam packed with secrets, tips and strategies. It's also filled with plenty of examples to show you how these strategies work in the real word. The following is a brief summary of what you will learn in each chapter:

Chapter 2: Where to Find Great Scholarships. Before you can win a scholarship you need to find them. This chapter shows you the best places to find scholarships and also how to select the awards that you have the best chance of winning.

Chapter 3: Judges' Roundtable: Inside the Selection Process. Meet actual judges and understand from their perspective what it takes to win scholarships.

Chapter 4: Essay Writing Workshop. In this information-packed chapter we give you everything you need to craft a powerful essay. We guide you step-by-step from selecting a topic to using effective writing techniques to avoiding common mistakes.

Chapter 5: 30 Winning Scholarship Essays. See how strategy is put into action in these essays that won $3 million in scholarships. See how your essay compares and be inspired by these successes.

Chapter 6: 12 Essays That Bombed. The best lessons often come from failure—and preferably the failure of someone else! These disaster essays illustrate important lessons of what not to do in the essay.

Chapter 7: Judges' Roundtable: The Scholarship Essay. Many of the scholarship judges have read hundreds if not thousands of essays and know what works and what doesn't. See what the judges have to say about the making of a winning essay.

Chapter 8: Winning Interview Strategies. Learn how to deliver a knockout interview. Discover what every good interviewee knows and how to overcome interview nervousness.

Chapter 9: Real Interview Questions & Answers. Preview typical interview questions and review example responses to learn what makes a powerful answer.

Not Just Looking for Straight A Students
Scholarship Program Considers Other Factors

You might think that scholarships seek only students with perfect SAT scores and flawless GPAs. This is not true. Many scholarships including those awarded by an international financial institution are looking beyond grades and test scores.

For this scholarship, the judges look at many factors besides grades, and test scores are not even requested in the application.

"We believe that success in life is more than a GPA. It's also what you can accomplish in your personal life and in your community," says Shirley Kennedy Keller.

Keller encourages all students to apply, even those with less than perfect academic records or test scores. "This scholarship applies to virtually every high school junior who has a B minus to C plus grade point average who wants to continue their education or training beyond high school. That hopefully provides some encouragement to students who say that scholarships don't apply to me," she says.

The message is clear: If you don't have perfect grades or test scores, don't let that prevent you from applying for awards.

Chapter 10: Judges' Roundtable: The Interview. Find out what the judges are really listening for when they interview you.

Chapter 11: Final Thoughts. A few final tips before you embark on the journey to winning free cash for college.

Why We Know So Much about Scholarships

You may be wondering who we are and what we know about winning scholarships. As the authors of several books on college admission and scholarships including *The Ultimate Scholarship Book, Get Free Cash for College, 1001 Ways to Pay for College* and *Get into Any College,* we have had the unique opportunity to meet thousands of students and scholarship judges. In writing this book we conducted extensive research and interviewed dozens of scholarship judges and scholarship-winning students. We have distilled all of this research into the easy-to-read pages of this book.

But just as important as the research that went into this book is the fact that we've been where you are today. Both before and during college we were fanatical about applying for scholarships. Using the strategies that we have incorporated into this book, we won more than $100,000 in merit-based scholarships. This money was instrumental in allowing us to graduate from Harvard University debt-free.

In addition, we have served as scholarship judges for numerous competitions. One scholarship that we judge is the SuperCollege.com Scholarship, which receives over 10,000 applications each year. Reading these application essays has given us valuable experience, and we have seen what works as well as what mistakes students make over and over. We are also expert interviewers, having conducted both scholarship interviews and admission interviews for Harvard.

The sum total of this experience, research and know-how is contained within these pages. If you follow these strategies, you too can become a scholarship winner. Always remember that someone is going to win every scholarship that is out there, and there is no reason for that someone not to be you.

CHAPTER TWO

WHERE TO FIND GREAT SCHOLARSHIPS

In this chapter:

■ Scholarship goldmines

■ How to decide which scholarships to apply to and which to avoid

■ How to uncover the mission of any scholarship

Exploring Scholarship Goldmines

When we were looking for scholarships, we found them in nearly every place imaginable. We discovered some in the dusty collection of books at our library, others by serendipitous newspaper announcements of past winners. We even found an award advertised on a supermarket shopping bag.

Having personally spent hundreds of hours scouring the planet for scholarships and meeting hundreds of other successful scholarship winners, we have learned where most scholarships are hidden. To help make your scholarship hunt more efficient, we present what we believe are the best places to look for scholarships.

As you search, keep in mind that not every scholarship you find is one you should apply for. As the list of possibilities grows, evaluate each award to determine if it is right for you. Don't worry—we'll show you how to do this later in the chapter. But knowing which awards to pass on is vital since it lets you focus your time and energy on those awards that you have the best chance of winning.

The first two obvious places to find scholarships are:

Books. There are a number of good scholarship books from which to choose. When looking for a guide, seek one that offers detailed descriptions of the awards. Most importantly, make sure that the book has an easy-to-use index. You don't have time to read through every scholarship, so an index will help narrow your choices quickly. For example, our scholarship directory *The Ultimate Scholarship Book* not only contains thousands of awards but also has indexes based on criteria like field of study, ethnicity, athletics, hobbies, talents and much more to help you pick awards that match your talents and abilities.

Internet Websites. A great way to find scholarships is through the Internet. One of the benefits of online scholarship databases is that they can be updated often. Check out the free scholarship search on our website at www.supercollege.com. By creating a personal profile you can let our database do the work of finding awards that match you. Here are some websites we recommend to help you get started:

- SuperCollege (www.supercollege.com)
- Sallie Mae (www.salliemae.com/scholarships)
- MoolahSPOT (www.moolahspot.com)
- The College Board (www.collegeboard.com)
- Scholarships.com (www.scholarships.com)
- AdventuresinEducation (www.aie.org)
- CollegeNet (www.collegenet.com)
- Chegg (www.chegg.com/scholarships)

Regardless of which websites you use, always make sure that they are free, (i.e. there are no fees for using the service). Never pay to do an online scholarship search.

While scholarship books and online databases are easy ways to find scholarships, you also need to do your own detective work. With literally millions of scholarships available it is impossible for any one book or website to list them all.

We believe that one of the best places to find scholarships is right in your own backyard—your community. Start with the following:

Counselor or financial aid officer. Do this right now. Call your counselor or financial aid officer and make an appointment. Before the meeting, determine how much money you will need for college and prepare a resume or list of your activities and awards. During the meeting explain your situation and ask if there are any scholarships that your counselor or advisor can recommend. These counselors and financial aid officers probably know more about the awards available in the community and on campus than anyone else. But, it is up to you to take the initiative to meet with them and give them enough information so they can recommend appropriate awards.

It's important whenever you speak to a counselor (either in high school or college) that you inquire about any scholarships that require a nomination. With these competitions, the applicant pool is almost always smaller. The most difficult hurdle is that you need to get nominated. You have nothing to lose by asking, and if nothing else, it shows how serious you are about financing your education.

Ambassadors Wanted

Scholarship Program Sought Cultural Representatives

Designed to promote international understanding, this scholarship program assisted more than 30,000 men and women from 100 nations since the program began in 1947.

"We're looking for the people who want to give something back to the community, people who we hope will make a difference in the world," says Russ Hobbs, a district scholarship chairman in the San Francisco Bay Area. "We're not looking for someone who will go back to their community or company and not give anything back."

Previous recipients in Hobbs' district have included an aspiring politician who speaks five languages, a former teacher who has interned with the United Nations and the holder of a patent for a shallow water pump.

One of the reasons why recipients of the award must be committed to making a difference is that they are ambassadors representing their home country abroad. As a part of the program, scholars make presentations about their home country in the countries in which they study.

Brent Drage says that the organization seeks people who will "represent our culture and appreciate the culture they are visiting." These are also qualities that are valued by club members.

And the organization hopes that scholars who return stay involved with the program, speaking to future applicants and even becoming organization members themselves.

Activities. Many clubs and organizations on campus offer awards for their members. Meet with the officers or advisors to see what is available. Also check with the national parent organization, if the group has one, since it may also provide scholarship funds.

Professional associations. One or more professional associations exist for practically every career field. These groups often offer awards for students in their field. For example, the American Dental Association and American Medical Association provide scholarships for students who want to become future dentists and doctors. If you have a strong idea of what you want to do after college, these professional associations can be a real gold mine of scholarships.

Community organizations. You don't have to belong to an organization to win a scholarship. In fact, many community groups raise money with the intent of giving it away to members of their community who are prospective students. Local Elks clubs, American Legions and Lions clubs often offer scholarships for outstanding students in the community. These groups view their scholarship programs as part of their service to the community. Look up the 10 largest organizations in your area and contact them.

Hometown professional sports team. Is your city the home of a professional sports team? If so contact the front office to see if they offer scholarships. Many teams offer scholarships that have nothing to do with athletic ability. You can also visit the official website of your hometown professional teams and look for a "community," "foundation" or "player's foundation" link.

Employer. If you have a full- or part-time job, check with your employer for awards. Many companies offer educational support as an employee benefit. If your employer doesn't offer a scholarship, suggest that they start one.

Parents' employer. Companies often award scholarships to the children of their employees. Ask your parents to speak with their human resources department about scholarships and other educational programs offered to employees and their families.

Parents' union. Many unions also sponsor scholarships for the children of their members. Again, have your parents speak with the union officers about union-sponsored scholarships and other educational programs.

Church or religious organizations. Religious organizations may provide scholarships for members. Inquire both locally at your house of worship as well as with the national organization, if any.

Local government. Often, local city council members and state representatives have a scholarship fund for the students who live in their districts. Even if you didn't vote for them, call their offices and ask if they offer any scholarships.

Local businesses. Local businesses often provide awards to students in the community. Start inquiring at your local Chamber of Commerce or similar business organization.

Local newspaper. Most community newspapers make announcements about local students who win scholarships. Keep a record of the scholarship announcements or look at back issues of the newspaper. Check last year's spring issues and you'll probably find announcements of scholarship recipients. Contact the sponsoring organizations to see if you're eligible to enter the next competition.

After you have exhausted the resources in your own community, you can then expand your search to your entire state or even the nation. Many large corporations offer scholarships (think: Coca-Cola, Microsoft, Burger King, Dell, etc.). Fortunately, most of these larger state-wide and nation-wide awards will be listed in scholarship books and on websites. The downside is that there will be a lot of competition for these awards.

Work Experience & Financial Aid
Program Assists Students Throughout College

Students who become scholars for this media company not only receive a $40,000 scholarship, they also receive four summer internships and a full-time job after they graduate from college.

Nominated by one of the local media outlets, scholars are selected in their senior year of high school. Even before they start college, the students work at a 12-week internship during the summer between their senior year of high school and freshman year of college. For the next three summers, the students intern and then work for the company for one year after they graduate.

"It's building a relationship between students and the company early on at a time when students want to learn more about the media industry," says Jacqui Love Marshall, vice president of human resources, diversity and development.

In addition to the internships and job opportunity, the students also meet annually at a Scholars Retreat. The retreat allows the students to meet executives of the company, interact with each other and gain additional training. A recent retreat brought the students to a national industry conference and offered the students additional workshops on subjects such as workplace political skills, business social skills and strategic planning in the media industry.

"For us it's a great opportunity to find new talent. For students it's a wonderful opportunity for them to get a diverse experience before graduating," Marshall says.

Which Scholarship Is Right for You?

Recently, a student wrote to us with a problem. He had conducted a search for scholarships on the Internet. Anticipating that he would find a handful of awards to apply for, he was shocked to find not handfuls but bucketfuls—more than 100 potential scholarships. Unless he made applying for scholarships his full-time job, there was no way that he could apply for all of them.

You will likely find yourself in a similar situation. Since there are so many scholarships available, the problem may not be finding awards but deciding which ones you have the best chance of winning. Although

When & Where to Find Scholarships
SallieMae.com

The best advice that Michael Darne, director of business development for Sallie Mae, has for students is to start early and use both high and low tech search tools.

"It really helps to start early. Students should begin thinking about scholarships in their sophomore year," recommends Darne. Even if you are not able to apply for every award that you find, keeping a running list now will give you a huge advantage once you become a senior.

As for where to find scholarships, Darne recommends two distinctly different methods. "You can use a scholarship search engine like the Sallie Mae search engine," says Darne. But besides the Internet, Darne also advises to not overlook the people around you.

"Meet with your guidance counselor. They're going to know about most of the good local scholarships. Get the word out to everyone you know that you're going to college and you need the money. Some of these scholarships may not be big money, but $500 here or $1,000 there can add up quickly," he says.

there is no way to predict if you will win a scholarship, there are some techniques you can use to select those that fit you best and therefore offer you the best chance of winning. Naturally, these are the ones for which you should apply.

The key is to realize that almost every scholarship organization has a mission or goal for giving away its money. Few groups give away free money for no reason. For example, a nature group might sponsor a scholarship with the goal of promoting conservation and encouraging students to be environmentally conscious. To this end the group will reward students who have demonstrated a concern for the environment and have some plan to contribute to this cause in the future.

Understanding the mission of the scholarship is important because it will clue you into the kind of student the organization is interested in finding. If you have the background, interests and accomplishments that match this mission, then it is a scholarship you have a good chance of winning.

In our example of the nature group, if you are passionate about conservation, are active in an organization like the Sierra Club and know that you could write a compelling essay about your interest in global warming, then you would be a great candidate. If, on the other hand, you can't remember the last time you spent more than an hour outdoors, this award is not for you and you would be wasting your time by applying.

By understanding the mission of the scholarship, you can determine if you are the kind of student the organization wants to reward.

Make Learning Their Mission Your Mission

There is no mystery to figuring out why organizations give away money. In most cases, the organizations come right out and tell you what they are trying to achieve with the award.

Start by carefully reading the award description. Oftentimes organizations spell out what they are looking for in the description of who is eligible for the award. Sometimes they provide the criteria that they use for judging the competition. Criteria can include qualities such as academic achievement, community involvement, leadership, specific career goals and character.

These requirements are valuable clues. Is there a minimum GPA? If there is and it's high, then academic achievement is probably important. Does the application provide a half page to list your activities? If so, then your involvement in organizations and projects outside of school is probably a fairly significant part of the selection criteria. Do you need to submit an essay on a specific topic or a project to demonstrate your proficiency in a field of study? All of these requirements are clues about what the scholarship committee thinks is important. Visualize yourself filling out their application. Would you have enough information to fill all of the blanks and answer all of the questions? If not, then you may want to consider passing on this award to focus on one that you are more qualified to win.

After reading the application, research the awarding organization. What is the group's mission? Who are its members? What do they hope to accomplish? You can probably guess what kind of student will impress a group of physicists versus poets. All things being equal, most clubs and organizations want to reward students who are most similar to their membership. If you don't know much about the organization, contact them to find out more. Check out their website. Read their brochures or publications. The more you know about why the organization is giving the award, the better you'll be able to understand how you may or may not fit with their expectations.

For a local scholarship you may actually know the previous winner. If you do, definitely contact him or her and learn as much as you can about the selection process. Ask for advice. Don't forget to ask winners why they think they won. Often, their familiarity with the contest and experience of having gone through the competition will give them an impression of why they were selected.

Making the Match

As your list of scholarships grows, you need to start prioritizing. Create an ordered list with the scholarships that fit you best written at the top. As you find new scholarships, you can decide where in the list they should go. When you start to complete applications, just start at the top of the list and work your way down. (Don't forget to list the deadlines since this may affect the order in which you list the awards.) The goal is not to get through the entire list but to get through as many as possible while still allowing enough time to create a quality application for each competition.

Prioritizing not only gives you an easy way to approach each competition but it also forces you to really think about what the scholarship committee is looking for. You will want to ask critical questions such as these:

- Do you have the background to fit with the expectations of the committee?
- Are your talents synonymous with those necessary to win?
- Have you accomplished tasks or won awards that show achievement in the area of the award?

You also avoid wasting time on awards that at first glance sound good (perhaps they have huge prizes) but you really have no chance of winning.

Finding awards that match your background, achievements and interests is extremely important. All of the essay and interview strategies presented in the following chapters are most effective if you have spent time selecting awards that are a match to your qualifications.

CHAPTER THREE

JUDGES' ROUNDTABLE: INSIDE THE SELECTION PROCESS

In this chapter:

- Get the inside scoop from real scholarship judges and experts

- Discover how the selection process actually works

- See who judges the competitions

- Understand what makes the difference between being a winner and a runner-up

Meet the Scholarship Judges

This is the first of three Judges' Roundtables in this book. We present these candid conversations with actual scholarship judges and experts so that you can hear in their own words what works and what doesn't.

Imagine that you were trying to win $1,000. One way to do this would be to buy a lottery ticket. Another way would be to apply for a scholarship. The difference between the two is that you cannot affect your chances of winning the lottery, but you can affect your chances of winning a scholarship.

When applying for scholarship competitions, one of the most important things to understand is why the organization is giving the award. Every organization has a reason for providing funds to students. These reasons can be quite varied. The organization may want to contribute to the communities in which it does business, increase the status of members of a minority or underrepresented group or build morale among its employees.

By understanding what the organization hopes to achieve through its scholarship program, you can develop essays and interview answers that best show how you fulfill the mission of the award. Here are some examples of purposes of scholarship programs. Try to imagine that you are applying to these awards and think about how knowing the purpose of each scholarship would help you to create a better application.

Q What is the purpose of your award? Why are you giving away free money?

Georgina Salguero
Hispanic Heritage Awards Foundation
"Our mission is to promote and reward Hispanic excellence and to provide a greater understanding of the contribution of Hispanic Americans in the U.S. One way we do this is through identifying and rewarding outstanding youth who in turn will serve as the role models for other youth.

"In addition to a scholarship award, we also provide each winner with a $1,000 check to donate to an established nonprofit organization of the student's choice. This is a way for the student to give right back to the community, to never forget who they are and where they came from. After all, how many 17-year-olds do you know who have a way to thank the community that has helped them get to where they are?"

Cathy Edwards
Discover Financial Services Inc.
"We wanted to structure a program that would not only demonstrate our commitment to education but also invest in our children's futures."

Ellen Frishberg
Johns Hopkins University
"The Hodson award goes to students who present the best credentials in our incoming class academically and in leadership. We're looking not just for local leadership but leadership on a regional or national level."

Brent Drage
Rotary International Ambassadorial Scholarship Program
"Our scholarship program was started to further international understanding by providing money for students to study abroad. That's why we call our winners ambassadors. Recipients are expected to be ambassadors of good will."

Tracey Wong Briggs
All-USA Academic Teams
"Our program is really an editorial project for *USA Today*. What we are trying to do is tell the stories about what outstanding students can do. We are looking to reward students who have a good story to tell about something they have accomplished either academically or extracurricularly."

Marie M. Ishida
California Interscholastic Federation Scholar-Athlete of the Year
"We want to acknowledge and recognize outstanding scholars who are also good athletes."

Jacqui Love Marshall
Knight Ridder Minority Scholars Program
"We're looking to find people early in their career planning who have an interest in newspapering, either journalism or working on the business side. We also want to raise interest and awareness about careers in newspapers among students."

Corisa Moreno
The Music Center Spotlight Awards
"Our award is meant to encourage high school students in the visual and performing arts to continue to follow their passion by providing support."

Wanda Carroll
National Association of Secondary School Principals
"We administer several awards that have different goals. For example, the Prudential Spirit of Community Award seeks to identify and honor middle level high school students on the basis of their volunteer work. For Wendy's High School Heisman Award we are looking to honor and promote both citizenship and athletic ability. For the Principal's Leadership Award we want to recognize an outstanding student leader."

Bob Murray
USA Funds
"Our scholarship program is aimed toward lower-income students in an attempt to narrow the gap in college attendance rates between lower-income and higher-income families."

Q Who typically judges the scholarship competition?

When applying for scholarships, it's important to keep in mind who the judges are. If you know that the judges will be local leaders, you may focus on how you have contributed to the community. If you can, ask who will be on the selection committee. This may help you select which essay subject and interview topics of conversation are the most appropriate.

Georgina Salguero
Hispanic Heritage Awards Foundation
"Within the 12 cities of our regional competition we try to get local leaders to be the judges. For example, we work with the head of the chamber of commerce, people at various universities, clergy, civic leaders and other leaders within the community. We feel that these people know best how to evaluate the students in their communities."

Tracey Wong Briggs
All-USA Academic Teams
"For the high school competition, the judges include representatives from the National Education Association and National Association of Secondary School Principals. For the college competition, the judges include representatives from the American Council on Education, National Association of Independent Colleges and Universities, American Association of Colleges for Teacher Education and a former winner."

Laura DiFiore
FreSch! Free Scholarship Search
"I try to get a diverse group of people. Recent judges have included an Episcopalian minister, nurse, former librarian, substitute teacher, accountant, retired homemaker, computer programmer and high school junior."

Jacqui Love Marshall
Knight Ridder Minority Scholars Program
"We form our judging committee with two or three people at the corporate office level, sometimes a person from our local newspaper (*The San Jose Mercury News* or a Monterey newspa-

per) and then I usually ask someone from the community or local industry. Each year I aim to create a diverse committee."

Russ Hobbs
Rotary International Ambassadorial Scholarship Program
"We have a six-member judging panel. Three are former Ambassadorial Scholars. The other three are Rotarians who have a love of the scholarship program."

Q How does your scholarship selection process work?

Understanding how the selection process works as well as realizing that not all competitions are the same will help you see where to focus your energies. If you can, learn about the scholarship program's selection process, what happens at each stage and how the applicants are evaluated.

Kimberly Hall
United Negro College Fund
"Students submit their applications directly to the UNCF. We perform a preliminary screening and send the strongest applications that we feel match the goals of specific donors on to those donors. Typically, the donor will then select the winner."

Trisha Bazemore
Coca-Cola Scholars Foundation
"The foundation first selects semifinalists based on a quantitative analysis of students' initial applications. Then, a 27-member Program Review Committee reviews the semifinalists' applications and essays. From this judging, 250 students are advanced as finalists. These students are then asked to travel to Atlanta at the expense of the Scholars Foundation to attend the Scholars Weekend, where they meet the other finalists and are interviewed by members of the National Selection Committee. Based on their applications and this interview, finalists are designated either as one of 150 Coca-Cola Scholars, receiving a four-year, $20,000 scholarship or as one of 150 Regional Finalists, receiving a four-year, $4,000 scholarship."

Corisa Moreno
The Music Center Spotlight Awards
"We start with our preliminary audition and there we screen for the basics. For example, let's say you're a singer. We would look for basic skills like tone and pitch. For dance we would look at the quality of your dance skills and musicality. As the applicants advance, the competition gets more intense because you've got a handful of very qualified dancers and musicians. At the final level everyone is extremely talented and what often makes the winner stand out is that extra level of professional persona."

Tracey Wong Briggs
All-USA Academic Teams
"We have two steps. The preliminary judges score each applicant against a score sheet. That's why it's real important for people to read the nomination form carefully since every item on the nomination form is what we are judging for on the score sheet. During the finals, the judges meet and they try to build an academic team. They read all of the finalist applications and pick the first, second and third teams."

Wanda Carroll
National Association of Secondary School Principals
"When you are dealing with thousands of applications, you have to find a way to narrow the field. All of the applications are screened using an algorithm. We determine a set number of criteria that they have to meet and a certain number of points that they need to have to be considered for the finals. We narrow down our applicants to the top 1,000 or 2,000 applications. Each application is then read by a team of readers. A team will select a state and read all of the applications from that state. The number of awards for a specific state is based on the population of that state."

Laura DiFiore
FreSch! Free Scholarship Search
"There are two stages for the judging. I personally pull out the no go's. These are the applicants that on first glance are clearly not qualified to move forward in the competition. Those that pass this stage are sent to judging. During the judging stage you have to impress all 10 judges. We use a point scale, and the

winning applicant and essay has received the highest marks from all of the judges. We usually pick out the winner in about three hours. The second and third prizes tend to take us two days. Out of all the entries, there will be about 50 stories and 70 poems going to final judging."

Q What qualities do you look for when selecting the winner?

If you know what qualities the organization is seeking in the winner, you can highlight those achievements that best showcase these qualities. Carefully read the organization's literature, website and publications to figure out what the judges seek. Or contact the organization directly to ask. Imagine how much stronger your application will be if you apply for these awards and know what the judges themselves think is most important.

Bob Murray
USA Funds
"In addition to the income requirement, we consider past academic performance and future potential, leadership, participation in school and community activities, work experience and career and educational aspirations and goals. Each of these additional criteria carry approximately equal weight."

Trisha Bazemore
Coca-Cola Scholars Foundation
"We are primarily looking at overall achievements in leadership, not only in school activities but also within their communities."

Georgina Salguero
Hispanic Heritage Awards Foundation
"Because the students select from seven career or talent categories in which to enter, the selection committee asks, 'Do we see this student excelling in this category 10 years from now?' With any selection, the cream rises to the top. We look at their academics, community service, leadership, as well as their fit and potential within their category."

Jacqui Love Marshall
Knight Ridder Minority Scholars Program
"We're looking for primarily academic strength. This is a person who is likely to do well in college so they won't be struggling. We also want a person who has a genuine interest in either journalism or the newspaper business."

Cathy Edwards
Discover Financial Services Inc.
"We're asking students to not only list community service efforts but to describe why they've been meaningful. It makes them stop and reflect. It helps them demonstrate their well-roundedness. It's not the students who have the highest GPA. We're trying to help the students who might not have scholarship dollars available to them."

Tracey Wong Briggs
All-USA Academic Teams
"The judges are looking for how you use your intellectual skills outside of the classroom, how you take academic excellence beyond getting an 'A' in class. Judges ask things like how are you using the knowledge that you're gaining in the classroom? Do you have a rigorous curriculum and are you challenging yourself?"

Corisa Moreno
The Music Center Spotlight Awards
"We look at the end result. Our past finalists are at a very professional level. A lot of them go on to major dance companies and institutions such as Juilliard. They are at that professional level where you could stick them on a stage anywhere and they would be a crowd pleaser."

Laura DiFiore
FreSch! Free Scholarship Search
"We're looking for originality and creativity, what we call the goosebump effect. When you get to the last sentence of the essay, you lean back and say 'wow.'"

Wanda Carroll
National Association of Secondary School Principals
"The National Honor Society Scholarships are based on the students' character, service and leadership as exemplified in their application and essay. As the name suggests, winners for the Principal's Leadership Award are selected based on their leadership. Our selection committee seeks a student who is class president, who is involved in athletics being captain or co-captain or who demonstrates community service as the head of their youth group. In short we are looking for someone who is obviously showing leadership qualities. The Prudential Spirit of Community Award, on the other hand, is based entirely on community service. One recent winner started a *Suitcases for Kids* program to provide suitcases for children in homeless shelters to move their belongings."

Russ Hobbs
Rotary International Ambassadorial Scholarship Program
"We're not looking for that person who has a 4.0 GPA and spends all his time in the library. We're looking for the people who want to give something back to the community, people who we hope will make a difference in the world and who believe in the values that we believe in Rotary. It's our hope that at some point in the future our winners will become Rotarians."

Q What sets the winner apart from the runner-up?

One of the most frequent observations from scholarship judges is that there are many more students qualified to win than there are scholarships available. This means that they must look for that little something extra to separate the winners from the almost winners. Here is some guidance to help you understand what can set you apart from the other applicants.

Shirley Kennedy Keller
American Association of School Administrators
"It's about what the students have accomplished in more than just one area of their lives. We believe that success in life is more than a GPA. It's also what you can accomplish in your

personal life, in your community. We're looking for the best all-around applicants. We're looking for students who are going to be successful in their lives."

Corisa Moreno
The Music Center Spotlight Awards
"They really have to enjoy what they're doing. That comes off quite a bit in their performances. You can see when they have a deep love for their art form."

Brent Drage
Rotary International Ambassadorial Scholarship Program
"Students who have a little more concrete plan tend to edge out others who don't. We understand that at that age you need to be flexible about your future, but we also want to see that you have some grasp on where you're headed."

Q What advice do you have for future applicants?

Some of the best advice you can get is from those who will be judging your scholarship applications. Since many have seen hundreds if not thousands of applications, they see firsthand how you can find awards, create a powerful application and essay and avoid the mistakes that other students make.

Kimberly Hall
United Negro College Fund
"Start looking for scholarships and applying early. I encourage students to start in their sophomore year of high school. Of course, they can start even earlier than that too."

Tracey Wong Briggs
All-USA Academic Teams
"Pursue the interests you love. One of the things we see is students who just care so much about what they're doing. If you do that, the awards will come."

Mario A. De Anda
Hispanic Scholarship Fund
"Read the application before you start filling it out. Spend time on the personal statement. It's our first impression of you so it needs to be good."

Wanda Carroll
National Association of Secondary School Principals
"There is nothing that disqualifies a student quicker than not following instructions. Make sure that all the signatures are there. Make sure you have every 'i' dotted and every 't' crossed. We have hundreds each year who don't make the first cutoff. It's not that they are not qualified but they just haven't followed the instructions."

Russ Hobbs
Rotary International Ambassadorial Scholarship Program
"Sell us on the things that you have done outside of the academic area. You need to let us know why we should want to fund you over 30 or 40 other candidates in our district."

Ellen Frishberg
Johns Hopkins University
"Focus and do well. We're looking for the academic program not just grades. We also want to see that students do well in activities and that they don't just join lots of organizations for the sake of listing them on their application. Focus on leadership since this award tends to go to students who invented, chaired, captained or did something that shows leadership."

Laura DiFiore
FreSch! Free Scholarship Search
"The bottom line is that we want to give you the money. It's up to you to give us a reason to say 'yes.' Please, please, please give us reasons to say 'yes.'"

Participating Judges & Experts

Trisha Bazemore, Program Assistant, Coca-Cola Scholars Foundation

Tracey Wong Briggs, Coordinator, *USA Today* All-USA Academic and Teacher Teams

Wanda Carroll, Program Manager, National Association of Secondary School Principals

Mario A. De Anda, Director of Scholarship Programs, Hispanic Scholarship Fund

Laura DiFiore, Founder, FreSch! Free Scholarship Search Let's Get Creative Short Story and Poetry Scholarship Contest

Brent Drage, Resource Development Assistant, Rotary International Ambassadorial Scholarship Program

Cathy Edwards, Manager, Public Relations and Charitable Sponsorships, Discover Financial Services Inc.

Ellen Frishberg, Director of Student Financial Services, Johns Hopkins University

Kimberly Hall, Peer Program Manager, United Negro College Fund

Russ Hobbs, District Scholarship Chairman, Rotary International Ambassadorial Scholarship Program

Marie M. Ishida, Executive Director, California Interscholastic Federation (CIF) Scholar-Athlete of the Year

Shirley Kennedy Keller, Program Director, American Association of School Administrators

Jacqui Love Marshall, Vice President of Human Resources, Diversity and Development, Knight Ridder Minority Scholars Program

Corisa Moreno, Project Coordinator, The Music Center Spotlight Awards

Bob Murray, Manager of Corporate Communications, USA Funds

Georgina Salguero, Senior Manager, Programs and Events, Hispanic Heritage Youth Awards

ESSAY WRITING WORKSHOP

In this chapter:

■ Why the essay is critical

■ What judges look for in the scholarship essay

■ The three common features of all money-winning essays

■ How to find the perfect topic

■ The keys to crafting a powerful essay

■ Why sob stories don't work

■ Hard to believe but true essay mistakes

■ How to recycle your essay

Why the Essay Is Critical to Winning

Let's imagine for a moment that you are a scholarship judge. You have an enormous pile of applications in front of you. From the application forms, you can get basic information about each applicant such as grades, test scores and brief descriptions of their activities.

But without being able to meet each candidate, how do you get a sense of who they are so that you can determine if they are the most deserving of your money? One of the best (and sometimes only) ways to get to know the applicants beyond their cut and dry statistics is through their essays.

This is why for many scholarship competitions the essay is the most important part of the application and where you should spend the most time. Scholarship judges view the essay as their window into who you are, your passions and your potential. It is their way of getting to know you without actually meeting you. And it is where you can make the strongest and most meaningful impression.

There are some interesting implications depending on the type of student that you are. If you are a straight "A" student with excellent test scores and a flawless academic record, you may be tempted to rely on these achievements to carry your application all the way to the final round. However, if you neglect the essay, your achievements (no matter how impressive) may advance you beyond the preliminary round, but you won't win the big prize.

On the other hand, if you are an average student and know that other applicants will have better academic achievements, you can use the opportunity that the essay provides to make yourself stand out. In many cases you will actually be able to beat applicants who have higher GPAs and test scores.

Regardless of your accomplishments and academic achievements, you need to write a powerful essay if you want to win a scholarship.

The Making of a Powerful Essay

Every summer there is a blockbuster adrenaline-laden action movie complete with pumped-up action hero, oversized guns and unbelievable

Focus on Solutions
United Negro College Fund

Some students seem to think that the more tears they can get the selection committee to shed, the better their chances will be to win. It's true that scholarship judges will feel sympathy for students who have gone through difficult times. But they will reward those who have done so and succeeded or who have a plan for succeeding despite these obstacles.

In the over 400 scholarship programs that the United Negro College Fund administers, essays play an important role. "It gives you a sense of who the student is and what they want to do with the money if they win. It gives you more of a picture of the student as a whole as opposed to just a name," says Kimberly Hall, peer program manager.

While many students write about serious issues or hardships, Hall advises students to take a positive approach when writing their essays. Instead of focusing only on their problems, students should explain what they have faced and then describe their plan of action for the future. The best essays have a sense of "purpose and direction," she says.

car chases. In the midst of exploding buildings and the hero tearing away in a red sports car, it would be out of place for the background music to be a polka. The sights and sounds need to fit together to create the desired atmosphere. If one element is out of place (like a polka during the climax of an action scene) it destroys the effect of the entire movie.

Similarly, what makes a good essay is that it fits within the context of the overall application. In other words, the essay and all other elements in your application package—such as your list of activities and teacher recommendations (if required)—must fit together to create the effect you want.

Let's say that you are applying for an award based on community service. In the application you list all of the community service groups that you belong to and service project awards that you've won. But in the essay you vent about your disgust for the homeless and how they should find jobs instead of blocking your passage on sidewalks. Your essay may be brilliantly conceived and written, but if its message is not in line with the rest of your application, it will create a conflicting message and keep you out of the winners' bracket.

Even if we reverse this example, the result is the same. Imagine that you wrote a brilliant essay about community service but had no related activities to back up the commitment you profess in the essay. The essay, no matter how well written, will not make up for a lack of actual involvement in community service work.

When you think about the essay, consider it within the context of the entire application. You want to present a cohesive message with the essay as the centerpiece. Each piece of the application should add to this unified message.

At this point many students ask, "How do I know what the message or theme of my essay and application should be?" The answer is actually quite simple and goes back to why you decided to apply for the scholarship in the first place.

> *The theme of your essay and application is almost always determined by the goal of the award or why the organization is giving away the money.*

For example, a minority advocacy organization may provide an award to help members of an under-represented ethnic group to pursue higher education. A private foundation may give an award to preserve the memory of a late benefactor who supported students entering teaching. A professional organization may award money to encourage students to enter their profession.

As you learned in Chapter 2, it's important to research and uncover the purpose of each award. Then you can use this information to guide the essay and application.

Once you know the goal of the organization, use that knowledge to choose which aspect of your life to highlight as the general theme of the essay. If you are applying for the award for under-represented students, you may want to focus on your potential and how you will be a role model for others in the future. To apply for the educator or other professional awards, you'd want to highlight your future in education or the field of the awarding organization. In other words, use the goal of the award as a guide for the essay.

Four Common Features of All Winning Essays

Let's imagine that you have done research on the scholarship organization and have a sense of what they hope to gain by giving away their money. You have even thought of a few themes that you could write about in the essay. No matter what topic you ultimately choose, there are qualities that are shared by all successful scholarship essays. It doesn't matter what type of student wrote the essay or what it is about, to write a winning essay you need to keep these points in mind.

#1 Originality

For your essay to be a winner, it needs to be original. Remember that your essay will be among thousands of other essays that are being judged. If your essay does not stand out, it will be forgotten along with your chances of winning.

There are two ways to be original. The first is to find a unique topic. Think about what makes you...well...*you*. What point of view or life experience can you share that is unique? One judge we know uses the "thumb test." Place your thumb over your name at the top of the essay, and ask yourself if any of your classmates could have written this essay. If the answer is "yes" then it fails the thumb test and is probably not original.

Unfortunately, finding a unique topic is very difficult, and that leads us to the second way that you can be original. Instead of racking your brains to come up with a 100% original topic, take an ordinary topic and approach it in an original way. For example, if you were writing about how your mother is a role model you would not want to approach it in the same way that everyone else will. Many applicants will write about how their mothers taught them the importance of education or showed them how to persevere in the face of adversity. If your essay is going to have any chance of winning, it needs to be different from those written by other competitors. So spend some time thinking–not

Hard to Believe But True Essay Mistakes
FreSch! Let's Get Creative Scholarship Contest

Laura DiFiore, the founder of FreSch! Free Scholarship Search, has seen many mistakes. Some have prompted her to separate essays into three piles: the good, the bad and the ugly. Those essays designated as the ugly are put into a box with a tombstone drawn on it.—Gen and Kelly

Bathroom humor. One applicant wrote an entire essay about excrement. "It met the requirements of originality but not creativity. It was gross."

Spelling mistakes. "While some mistakes are tolerated, if you can't spell your own major, you're not getting a scholarship."

Inferior, illegible printing. DiFiore received an essay in which the middle section of the applicant's printing ribbon ran out. This meant that she could only see the top third and bottom third of each letter. The entire middle of all of the letters was totally illegible.

Plagiarism. During a recent competition, DiFiore received essays from applicants who took last year's winning essay which was posted on her website, modified it and submitted it as their own.

Copycats. DiFiore received essays from three sisters who all wrote the same basic story.

Threats. One essay writer threatened the selection committee, "If you don't give me money I'm going to hunt you down."

Anonymous applicants. DiFiore has received applications with no name or address on them. It's difficult to award a scholarship to an anonymous applicant.

writing–about your mother. What is it specifically that she has done or said that has been so influential? Can you cite a concrete example? Maybe your mother has a secret recipe for meatloaf that she has shared with no one except you. Perhaps the moment that she revealed to you her treasured secret recipe was a milestone in your relationship. Focusing on this event and examining and analyzing it may yield a very powerful and certainly original essay. The truth is that we all have experiences and people that make us unique, and the key is to zero in on these and use them in your scholarship essays.

When you read the example essays in the next chapter, look at how each is unique. Pay special attention to how the authors present their topics. Notice how they often bring in points of view that help to make their essays original.

One sure way to ensure that your essay is original is to avoid common topics or approaches of other essay writers. In fact, these mistakes are so common that we have an entire chapter devoted to them. Be sure to carefully study the essays in Chapter 6, *12 Essays That Bombed*, to make sure that your topic or approach does not resemble any of these failures.

#2 Answer the Underlying Question

Have you ever been asked one question but felt like there was an underlying question that was really being asked? Maybe a parent has asked you something like, "Tell me about your new friend Karen." But what your parent is really asking is, "Tell me about your new friend Karen. Are her 12 earrings and tattoo-laden arms a sign that you shouldn't be spending so much time with her?"

In most cases the essay question is just a springboard for you to answer the real question the scholarship judges want addressed. An organization giving an award for students who plan to study business might ask, "Why do you want to study business?" But the underlying question they are asking is, "Why do you want to study business, and why are you the best future business person we should gift with our hard earned money?"

For every scholarship you will be competing with students who share similar backgrounds and goals. If you are applying to an award that supports students who want to become doctors, you can bet that 99% of the students applying also want to become doctors. Therefore, the goal of every scholarship judge is to determine the *best* applicant out of a pool of applicants who at first glance look very similar.

So let's distill the underlying question that the scholarship judges really want answered; that is, Why do you deserve to win? (Your answer should not be, "Because I need the money!")

Think about these two hypothetical essay topics: The Farmers Association asks about the future of farming. The Historical Society wants an analysis of the importance of history. While at first these two questions seem unrelated, they are both driving at the same thing: Tell us why you deserve to win.

In addressing either of these topics, you would need to recognize the underlying question. When writing the Farmers Association essay, you could discuss the general condition of farms and farmers, but you'd better be sure to include how you fit into the future of farming. Similarly when answering the Historical Society's question, you could write about history in any way that you please; but you should also include if not focus on your own past and future contributions to the field of historical research or preservation. Use the essay question as a way to prove to the scholarship committee that you are the worthiest applicant for the award.

#3 Share a Slice of Life

As you are explaining why you deserve to win, it is important that you also reveal something about yourself. Obviously, in the short space of 500 to 1,000 words you can't cover everything about you. This is why one of the most effective techniques is to share just a "slice of your life." In other words, don't try to explain everything. Just focus on one aspect of your life.

If you are writing about your involvement in an activity, it may be tempting to summarize your involvement over the years and list numerous accomplishments. However, this would sound more like a resume and it would not tell the judges something that they could not learn by reading your resume. However, if you focus on just one aspect or one day of an experience, you could spend some time below the surface and share something about who you are. In other words, you would be sharing a slice of your life.

Since many students write about activities in which they are involved, here are a few topics that you might want to consider. These will help you focus the essay and force you to share a slice of your life:

- What motivated you to get involved with this activity?
- How do you personally benefit from participating?
- How do you stay motivated during challenging times?
- Is there a person that you've met through this activity that has inspired you? How?
- What one accomplishment are you most proud of? Why?
- Have you ever considered quitting this activity? Why didn't you?
- What is one thing you learned from being involved?

These types of questions make you examine yourself and find a specific incident, moment or thought to share. Even if the subject of the essay is an activity that you enjoy, it is important that the judges who read it come away knowing more about you.

#4 Passion

As a student you have written a lot of essays. And let's be honest—most were probably on topics you didn't care much about. You might be tempted to approach the scholarship essay in the same way that you did when writing about the Roman Aqueducts, but this would be a tragic mistake. The last common feature of all winning essays is that they are written on subjects about which the author is truly passionate.

It is very difficult to fake passion for a subject. (Just try to be excited throughout your Uncle Larry's hourlong slideshow of his tonsil operation.) But when you are genuinely enthusiastic about something it does not take much effort for that energy to naturally show through in your writing. Therefore, when you are choosing a topic, be sure it is something you truly care about and are interested in. Without even trying, you will find that your sentences convey an excitement that the reader can almost feel.

When you read the examples in the next chapter, you will quickly see that the writers all cared deeply for their topics.

How to Find the Perfect Topic

When we were taught to color inside the lines, our artwork may have been neater but it was at the expense of creativity. The best time-tested method to develop creative ideas that lead to a great topic is through brainstorming. By thinking without restrictions, creativity flourishes. We have found that the best way to do this is to keep a notebook with you and write down ideas for topics whenever they pop into your head. Also set aside some time for a dedicated brainstorm session where you force yourself to generate new ideas.

When brainstorming topics don't be critical of the ideas you write down. Let your imagination roam. Also, ask your parents and friends for suggestions.

The one shortcoming of brainstorming is that sometimes a good idea does not make for a good essay. A thought may be too complex to write about within the limitations of the essay requirements.

The only way to really tell if an idea is good is to start writing. So from your list of ideas pick several that are the most promising and start composing an essay. Again, don't pay attention to the quality of the writing just yet. You are basically testing the topic to see if it has the potential to become a great essay.

If you get stuck and think the topic may not work then set it aside and try another. We have found that most students will try and then abandon two or three ideas for every good one they find. That means that you need a long list of ideas and must be willing to cut your losses and ditch a topic that does not pan out.

Putting Words onto Paper

At some point you can't escape the need to start writing. The best way to begin is the same as removing a bandage–just do it, and do it quickly. To help get you going, here are some strategies for writing:

Go beyond the Superficial
Getting Insight on Scholarship Sponsors

To apply for a scholarship program sponsored by a media company, students must write a personal statement. Many turn to the company's website to get background information on the company. For some, this is a mistake.

"You realize they went to the site and cut and pasted material from it into their essay. But it's clear that they have little idea what these facts mean," says Jacqui Love Marshall, vice president of human resources, diversity and development.

The students cite statistics about the number of media outlets owned by the company or the number of Pulitzer Prizes the media company has won. She adds, "It's almost the difference between writing a book report by having read the CliffsNotes versus having read the book."

What's more important than regurgitating statistics found on an awarding organization's website is finding a personal connection to the organization.

"When you're looking at dozens of these essays in the middle of the night, you begin to differentiate between someone who put their heart and soul in it, that there is a level of commitment there versus essays that have all the requisite information but not a personal involvement," says Marshall.

Remember to Focus on Originality. While it is not always possible to come up with an original topic—especially if the question is the same for everyone—make sure that the essay contains originality or that the topic is approached in a novel way.

If you are writing about involvement in a sport, don't use common topics like how sports taught you the value of teamwork or how you scored the winning touchdown, goal or point. These are repetitive topics. Using them risks having your essay lost among the hundreds of others that sound similar to yours. It's perfectly fine to write about common topics like sports, but think of a different angle. Maybe you had a unique experience or can focus on an aspect of athletics that is often overlooked.

Be Specific. A common mistake in essay writing is to use general statements instead of specific ones. Don't write, "Education is the key to success." Instead, give the judges a slice of your life. Show them how education has impacted your life in a single experience or realization.

If you are writing about your desire to become an astronaut you might explain how this began when your father bought you a model rocket for Christmas. Focusing on a specific example of your life will help readers relate to your experiences and ensure that your essay is memorable and (as a bonus) original.

Share Something Personal. While some questions ask about a national or international problem or event, the scholarship committee still would like to know something about you. After all, they are considering giving their money to you.

Some of the better essays written about serious issues like drug abuse or nuclear proliferation have also found ways to incorporate information about the author. One student who wrote about the U.S. arms policy spoke about his personal involvement in a club at school that hosts an annual peace conference. He was able to tie in the large international policy issues with the more personal aspect of what he was doing on an individual level. It was a great policy essay, which also revealed something about the author.

Have a Thesis. It sounds obvious, but many students' essays don't have a clear point. Whether you are describing the influence of your father or the effect of World War II on race relations, you must have a central idea to communicate to the reader.

To see if your essay has a central thesis, try this simple exercise. Ask yourself, "What is the point of my essay in a single sentence?" Here are some answers that would satisfy the question for essays on independence and drug addition, respectively:

"Growing up in the country taught me to be independent."

"Treatment of addiction is the only way to win the war on drugs."

If you cannot condense the point of your essay into a single sentence, then the main point may not be clear enough. Or worse, your essay may not have a thesis.

Expand on Your Accomplishments. Winning a scholarship is about impressing the judges and showing them why you are the best candidate for a monetary award. Your accomplishments, activities, talents and awards all help to prove that you are the best fit. Since you will probably list your activities on the application form, use the essay to expand on one or two of the most important ones.

However, don't just parrot back what is on the application. Use the opportunity to focus on a specific accomplishment, putting it into the proper context. Share details. Listing on the application that you were a stage manager for a play does not explain that you also had to design and build all of the sets in a week. The essay allows you to expand on an achievement to demonstrate its significance.

Beware of Meaningless Facts. Some students approach the essay like a research paper, cramming it with statistics and survey results. You might think that the facts and figures "wow" judges. While this does display research skills, facts and figures alone hardly make a good essay. In particular, if you are trying to impress a corporation with your knowledge of their sales and global markets, don't just repeat facts from their website. You may use facts about the sponsoring organization, but be sure that they are essential to the essay. Don't repeat statistics without a reason, and don't think that the more you have the better.

Use Examples & Illustrate

Mark R. Eadie, Coca-Cola Scholars Regional Winner

"Make sure to use examples to illustrate points. Instead of saying 'I was active in high school,' describe your high school activities. Also, focus on one or two activities that had special meaning to you.

"There's a fine line between bragging and too much humility. Be honest about yourself and what you've done, and the scholarship committee will recognize this. Your essay is going to be read by real people who are intelligent and wise so don't make things up. Trying to trick them is like trying to trick parents; it just doesn't work.

"Also, the essay readers may have to read hundreds of essays, so give them something to remember you by."

Avoid Clichés. We are all guilty of using a cliché in our writing. "Don't cry over spilled milk." "Good things come to those who wait." "Try and try and you will succeed." These are all common clichés. It's important to avoid using them in the essay. Why? First of all, the use of clichés is just lazy writing. You are using a common phase instead of taking the time to come up with your own words. Second it's not your words and therefore it's not original. When you use a cliché you are penalized for being both lazy and unoriginal. It's just not worth it. If you find yourself writing a cliché, stop, and rewrite the idea in your own words.

Don't Write a Sob Story. Tear-jerking stories may be popular subjects for television specials and song lyrics, but they rarely, if ever, win scholarships. A common theme students write about is why they need the scholarship money to continue their education. While this is a perfectly legitimate topic, it is often answered with an essay filled with family tragedies and hardships–a sob story. Again, there is nothing wrong with writing about this topic, but don't expect to win if the intent of your essay is to evoke pity.

If your main point (remember our test) is this: "I deserve money because of the suffering I've been through," you have a problem. Scholarship committees are not as interested in problems as they are in solutions. What have you accomplished despite these hardships? How have you succeeded despite the challenges you've faced? This is more significant and memorable than merely cataloging your misfortunes.

Plus, don't forget that to win you have to be an original. The sob story is one of the more common types of essays, and it is hard to compete when you are telling the same story that literally hundreds of other students are also writing. Remember that every applicant has faced difficulties. What's different and individual to you is how you've *overcome* those difficulties.

Show Positive Energy. Mom has probably said: "If you don't have anything nice to say, don't say anything at all." Everyone likes an uplifting story. Especially, since you have your entire future ahead of you, scholarship judges want to feel your enthusiasm. In fact, one reason adults love to volunteer to be scholarship judges is to meet positive and enthusiastic young adults who do not have the cynicism or closed minds of adults.

Try to stay away from essays that are overly pessimistic, antagonistic or critical. This doesn't mean that you have to put a happy spin on every word or that you can't write about a serious problem. But it does mean that you should not concentrate only on the negative. If you are writing about a problem try to present some solutions.

Your optimism is what makes organizations excited about giving you money to pursue your passion for changing the world. Don't shy away from this fact.

The Importance of Editors

There is an old writer's saying: "Behind every good writer is an even better editor." If you want to create a masterpiece, you need the help of others. You don't need a professional editor or even someone who is good at writing. You just need people who can read your work and provide useful and constructive feedback.

Roommates, friends, family members, teachers, professors or advisors all make great editors. When others read your essay, they will find errors that you missed and help make the essay clearer to someone who is not familiar with the topic.

You will find that some editors catch grammar and spelling mistakes but will not comment on the overall quality of the essay. Others will miss the technical mistakes but give you great advice on making the substance of your essay better. It's essential to find both types of editors.

As you find others to help improve your essay, be careful that they do not alter your work so much that your voice is lost. Editing is essential but your writing should always be your own.

Recycle & Reuse

Recycling in the context of this discussion has no relation to aluminum cans or newspapers. What we mean is that you should reuse essays that you have written for college applications, classes or even other scholarships. Writing a good essay takes a lot of time and effort. When you have a good essay you'll want to edit it and reuse it as much as possible.

Sometimes, to recycle an essay, you must change the introduction. Try experimenting with this. You may find that while you might have to write a few new paragraphs you can still use the body of the original essay.

One word of caution: Don't try to recycle an essay when it just doesn't fit. The essay must answer the question given by the scholarship organization. It's better to spend the extra time to write an appropriate essay than to submit one that doesn't match the scholarship requirements.

How to Write a Great Introduction or Conclusion

Great novels have two things in common—a gripping introduction and a conclusion that leaves the reader with something to think about. Great essays share similar traits.

The first impression that the judges get is from the introduction. If it does not catch their attention and make them want to read further then you will lose even before you have had a chance. Here are some strategies for beginning any essay:

Create action or movement. Use an example or short story to create action right at the beginning. Have you noticed how most movies begin with a striking scene that quickly draws you in? Do the same with your introduction.

Pose a question. Questions draw attention as the readers think about their answers and are curious to see how you answer them in the essay. You can also use an interesting or surprising fact in place of a question.

Use descriptions. If you can create a vivid image for readers, they will be more likely to want to read on. Just be sure to do so succinctly since you don't want the introduction to be filled with detail that does not move the plot forward.

Conclusions are just as important as introductions since they are the last impression you will leave with the reader (the scholarship judge). Here are a few tips for the closing remarks.

Be thoughtful. The conclusion should end with something insightful. You may even decide to withhold a thought from the essay so that you have something for the conclusion.

Essays Get Better with Each Revision
Kristin N. Javaras, Rhodes Scholar

"I highly recommend showing your essay to people who have won fellowships themselves or who have read successful fellowship application essays before (and the more people the better). I feel that the revision process was crucial for my essay: I went through about seven or eight drafts of my personal statement before I was satisfied!"

Don't just summarize. Since the reader has just finished the essay, there is no need for a restatement of the points that you made. It's okay to wrap up your thoughts in one sentence, but try to add to the conclusion as a whole by making an extra point.

Don't be too quick to end. Too many students tack on a meaningless conclusion or even worse, don't have one at all. Have a decent conclusion that connects with the rest of the essay and that doesn't consist of two words, "The End."

As you look at the essay ask yourself: Will they think about what I have said after they have finished reading? If the answer is yes, then you have written a conclusion that you can be proud of.

Stay Motivated

Writing scholarship essays may not be the ideal way to spend a Friday night or Sunday afternoon. But remember that these essays can win you hundreds, if not thousands, of dollars for college. Try to keep this in mind when you feel burned out. If you really get down on writing take a break. Go outside. Watch some meaningless television. Then when you are refreshed get back to your essay.

In the next chapter are the actual essays that won the writers thousands of dollars in scholarships. At some point each of these writers got tired or disgusted and contemplated quitting. But each persevered and didn't give up. They pushed ahead and finished their essays. If they had given up they would never have won the money that they did and that all important college diploma would have been a far more expensive (and for some impossible) accomplishment.

CHAPTER FIVE

30 WINNING SCHOLARSHIP ESSAYS

In this chapter:

- **30 real essays about challenges, family, issues, community service, career plans, leadership, academics, athletics and artistic talents**

- **Learn from and be inspired by these successful essays**

The Money-Winning Essays

You sit down at the computer, eyes focused on the monitor and fingers poised above the keyboard. You are ready to start writing your money-winning scholarship essay. But something is missing. Aha! What you need is inspiration.

In this chapter, we want to give you this inspiration. One of the best ways to learn how to write a successful essay is to read actual essays that won. While there is no single way to write a winning essay, most successful ones share traits such as originality, demonstrating why the author deserves to win and passion.

As you read these essays imagine that you are a scholarship judge. What image of the writer does the essay create? How do the essays make you feel? Would you give away your money to these writers?

Remember, unlike a creative writing assignment, the goal of a scholarship essay is to show the scholarship committee why you deserve to win. Keep in mind that these essays are meant to be examples of what worked for these particular students. Naturally, your essays will be individual to you. While your essays will surely differ in style, tone, language and subject matter, they should convey the same powerful impressions.

Ultimately, we want you to use these successful essays as inspiration to write your own masterpiece.

Experiences & Challenges

Brian C. Babcock, Marshall & Truman Scholarship Winner

The path to becoming a Marshall Scholar and Truman Scholar is a long one. Brian's journey began at Bowie High School in Bowie, Maryland, when he was elected the president of the Russian Club. Since that time, he has studied at the U.S. Military Academy at West Point and worked as a Russian linguist.

Brian is one of 40 students in the nation to win the Marshall Scholarship and one of 80 students to win the Truman Scholarship. With the Marshall Scholarship, he will study at Oxford after graduating. Brian plans to use the $30,000 Truman Award to support his future graduate studies in foreign service and history and would eventually like to become the Defense Attache to Russia, working with the governments of the former Soviet republics to assist them in dismantling their nuclear, biological and chemical weapons. In this essay for the Truman Scholarship, he describes how at age 17 he embarked on a hike of the Appalachian Trail from Maine to Georgia. The solo hike lasted six months.

Lessons from the Outdoors

The outdoors has always played a large role in my life, whether in Boy Scouts, on my own or with the military thus far. However, there is one outdoor experience of mine that did not involve my being in a club. I also did not get any awards for this experience, yet it has had a more profound impact on who I am than any other single event in my life, my "thru-hike" of the Appalachian Trail from Maine to Georgia.

I started my thru-hike when I was 17 years old, three weeks after I graduated from high school. It took me just over six months to complete. In those six months, I learned more about myself than in the previous 17 years or in the five years since. There is nothing with which it can compare.

I financed the hike with money that I saved during my last semester of high school, working 40 hours per week on top of my full-time student schedule. I was determined to reach Maine and hike south to Georgia. This was the first real goal that I had ever made for myself, and I reached it alone on a cold January morning.

The lessons from the trail are ones that have affected me in everything I have done since. Because of those six months, I see the world differently, in a way that is sometimes impossible to explain to someone else, though I might try.

Brian's contributions reflect his own opinions, not those of the U.S. military.

My life was not difficult growing up, but I found a need to put myself through the difficulties of trail life. From this time, I gained an appreciation for the little things, like clean water to drink and a dry place to sleep (both of which were sometimes lacking). I met people from all walks of life, as they crossed paths with my walk in life. From that experience I am better able to deal with those whose backgrounds do not resemble mine, a skill I have used often in the military.

Now I have turned my life 180 degrees. I no longer have hair to the middle of my back or a beard. I have traded my Birkenstock sandals for combat boots. Yet, somehow, everything I did on the trail applies to what I have done since. Whether it's suffering in a foxhole during field training, or sleeping in a cold, dank lean-to on my hike, the lessons are not all that different.

Though my journey in life has wandered back onto the beaten path, I know that if the nation needs me to lead soldiers into the brush or assist in providing humanitarian aid, I have my previous experience to draw from. Because I have been there, I have a common bond of suffering with millions throughout the world and another bond to all of my soldiers. I am still amazed at how my former life as a free-spirited wanderer has better prepared me for life as a disciplined soldier.

Daniel Heras, Scantron Scholarship Winner

Daniel dreams of becoming a teacher to inspire students to learn in the same way that he has been inspired by his teachers. In this essay, he describes one of the most meaningful experiences he has had in high school through the Environmental Science Club, which took him to real life locales to learn about science not from textbooks but from seeing, touching and experiencing science first hand. Student body president and captain of the baseball team at Woodrow Wilson High School in Los Angeles, Daniel won more than $17,000 in scholarships to attend U.C. Berkeley.

Inspired to Teach

In the ninth grade, I was introduced to the Environmental Science Club and to Mr. Quezada, my science teacher and advisor. Outside of the classroom and through the club, I saw an entirely different side to education. The science club took me to far and exotic destinations, such as the Islands of Hawaii, the underwater wonderlands of the Cayman Islands, the temperate climates of the Florida Everglades, the deep blue waters of the Mexican Riviera and the High Sierras of Northern California.

We learned that one cannot experience these things in class behind a small cramped desk made for 10-year-olds. I was able to hold, smell and sometimes taste, foreign artifacts. I have seen the migration patterns of the Humpback whale, have become a certified scuba diver, learned to surf, rock climb, snowboard and trail the mountains of the world, all while learning about science. Our trips have also given me the life skills of communication, learning to intermingle with people of the world.

It only took a year to see that teaching was my future. Why would someone not want to get paid for helping his or her community, to enlighten the future generation and best of all, do the things that bring joy to one's life all while on the job? I was given experiences I would not have received anywhere else, and I want to do the same for the next generation to come. There is a world that one can hold, smell and sometimes taste. I want to show people that there really is a world out there beyond the pictures in textbooks.

Mark R. Eadie, Coca-Cola Scholars Regional Winner

When Mark visits his 90-year-old grandmother, the two turn the volume on the television up. Though they are separated by almost 70 years in age, they share a similar problem: hearing impairment, Mark's grandmother because of age and Mark because of a childhood injury that left him partially deaf. This injury has not stopped Mark. If anything, it has sparked a passion to be a role model for others.

While a student at Columbia High School, Mark trained for hours as the lead of the school musical, perfecting his singing without the benefit of stereo hearing. The performance garnered rave reviews. From Rensselaer, New York, Mark received over $50,000 in scholarships to attend the University of Michigan, where he is a member of the national champion solar car team and is studying aerospace and mechanical engineering. He hopes that through his research in engineering he can develop solutions for others like him.

Invisible Handicap

Who would think a game of catch would change my life? At age 10 I lost hearing in one ear and had to struggle with the challenges resulting from this "invisible handicap." Through this I have become more sensitive to people's problems and handicaps, learned the value of my support community, refined career goals and challenged myself in new and difficult situations to help others.

My catching skills were not what my older brother thought, and his fast ball missed my glove and hit my cheek bone. After a severe concussion and cochlear surgery, I was totally deaf in the right ear. I had lost all stereophonic hearing and musicality. My voice started to become monotone. I could not tell from where sounds were coming, hear notes I was singing or distinguish voices in a noisy room. The hardest part was exhaustion from having to focus on everything going on. School became far harder. Conventional hearing aids don't work with total deafness, so I tried a microphone and receiver system in class. However, it was more frustrating than helpful. After that, my teachers were dazzled with my attentiveness, not realizing I was reading their lips. All this has been very tough emotionally.

A Scholarship Support Network
Emanuel Pleitez, Recipient of $30,000 in Scholarships

Emanuel Pleitez remembers falling asleep while writing his scholarship essays. In fact, he worked so late, that he went to the post office at the Los Angeles International airport to mail his applications because that was the only post office open until midnight. Fortunately, he had a classmate who joined him on these late night drives.

"You have to surround yourself with friends who are motivated like you, who want to go to college and apply for scholarships," he says.

Emanuel and his friend developed an informal support network for each other when applying for awards. He used his friend's computer because he didn't have one and the two helped edit each other's work. In fact, Emanuel encouraged his friend to apply for an award that he found. His friend ultimately won the award.

His classmate wasn't the only person that Emanuel relied on for help. He received encouragement from his coach, who was also his senior class advisor and school's dean. His counselor mentored him after Emanuel approached him during his freshman year of high school to explain his ambition to attend a selective college. He gained interviewing experience at a program he attended to prepare students for internships and essay-writing help from the Quest summer school program he attended at Stanford.

"I was really lucky to be surrounded by all these good people. At every stage there was always a couple of people who I could turn to for help," Emanuel says.

With my parents' help I learned not only to cope but to grow. Most people never know I have a severe hearing problem. I turn my head or move so they're on my "good ear" side. I ask people to clarify when statements are unclear. I still play sports, especially lacrosse, though my coach nearly goes hoarse yelling to me.

I challenged myself, joining symphonic band and chamber singers and taking a lead in "The Fantasticks" musical. Enormous hours were spent pinging on the piano, trying to match my voice to notes. The support of friends and teachers was wonderful, and we received rave reviews for the performances.

The struggle has brought me closer to my 90-year-old grandmother, who is losing her hearing. We visit daily and watch PBS together on weekends, the volume blasting. We empathize with each other, laughing and crying over the frustrations of deafness. When volunteering in the hospital cardiac care unit, I comfort older patients by comparing hearing aids. They laugh and do not feel quite so old.

Spring three years ago brought an incredible gift. A doctor developed a trans-cranial hearing aid. It transmits sounds powerfully from the deaf ear, through the skull, to the nerves in the "good" ear. Now, I hear some stereophonic sound and tonality. This cutting edge solution has helped me decide to study engineering, to help others as I have been helped. Engineering is a noble profession; its goal is to alleviate the human condition. I seek to examine and solve problems by creating new visions that combine innovation with technological development.

My invisible handicap makes communication difficult, but I wanted to help other youth grow and develop life skills, faith and values. So, I pushed myself and took increased leadership in Boy Scouts and in my church. These positions require good communication, making me work extremely hard. But the results have been worth the effort. As the leader of the Presbyterian Youth Connection Council for the Synod of the Northeast, I have worked with youth and adults from eight states. We hold training events to improve youth leadership. I went to Colorado to help the Synod of the Rocky Mountains establish a youth council. Twice we have planned conferences for nearly 200 youth. I have learned to work until a task is completed.

Though unable to say I'm glad it happened, I have benefited from my hearing loss. I have learned to use my limitations to help others and to never give up. My no longer monotone voice now reflects the non-monotone life I have developed.

Nhia TongChai Lee, Knight Ridder Minority Scholar

Nhia comes from a Hmong family where tradition is important. If his parents had their way, he would never date or even have friends of the opposite sex. While he respects his parents and his family's values, he feels that it's important that Hmong of his generation take steps toward independence and leadership. As he says, "Just make sure you take big steps and not little baby steps." And through writing he wants to be someone who influences those of his generation.

It's because of this desire to inspire others that Nhia got involved in his newspaper at Lansing Everett High School in Lansing, Michigan, and is now majoring in journalism at Michigan State University. His passion to affect others through his writing has been recognized. He has won more than $60,000 in scholarships including the Michigan State University Distinguished Freshman Achievement Award and *Detroit Free Press* Journalism Award. When asked his planned career field, he says that he will become the editor of *Rolling Stone.*

Only the Strong Survive

Our lives are not predetermined but rather a journey that each individual must decide for himself. Events that transpire along the way do not just disrupt the journey but sometimes occur to benefit it. During the Vietnam War, my family was forced out of their homeland Laos and into Thailand, where they sought refuge for five years. All was left behind to take a stab at giving my siblings and me a possible future. The only life they knew had been wiped clear of existence. The familiar air breathed, land cultivated and faces seen all seemed like a lost dream.

Relocating in Thailand did not manifest into the Promised Land everyone had heard about. Instead of the beautiful lands and abundance of food, what they found were crowded camps and no food. Hunger spread like wildfire and people died by the handful. What many thought was a safe haven was in actuality a waiting deathbed.

Only the strong survived the refugee camps. My family members were just more faces in the crowd of thousands in the same situation. It was there that I was born into a life deprived of the simple good things in life. Finding food was always a problem and just trying to survive to the next day was a top priority. My parents knew that in order to survive we had to leave the refugee camps. If you were lucky, you were sponsored to move to America. Along with thousands of others, we had nothing to do but wait. Wait for a reply to our pleas to leave.

In 1985 my family finally received word that our prayers out of Thailand were answered. A church in Michigan sponsored our family and that was our ticket out. We immigrated to the United States to start anew. We had to adopt a new language, a new culture and a whole new way of life. Through it all, we continued to practice our culture and customs. That was something my parents wanted to keep and pass on to generations to come. It was the only thing about the past that remained with us. My parents wanted us to grow up to be traditional Hmong boys and girls.

I knew what I wanted in life, but knowing that traditionally Hmong children married at a young age, it was hard to break out of that mold. By choosing journalism as a career path, I hope to set an example: following the traditional rules is not the only option, even though that's the only life we know. I want to complete school and have my writing reach a vast audience. I hope to make a difference with writing and show the youth of my culture that we can balance both worlds at the same time. We can still have respect for our parents and compassion for our culture while changing along with modern society. There is a lot more out there for us, a world beyond marriage and children, a world that can show a whole different perspective on life.

I want to show that growing up impoverished can still lead to being published in a national newspaper or writing a Pulitzer Prize-winning article. I want to be that role model for Hmong kids who sometimes feel trapped within the walls that are built around them.

I believe that if I can live my life the way I want it and not how my parents want it, then others can follow. Instead of marrying into a burden-filled life, I can become the anchor for that change. I want to take the path that my parents never spoke of. I know that in the end that will be the difference between what is and what could have been. Hopefully young people, not just Hmong kids, but anyone who feels lost can look at what I have achieved and find their own path.

Jennifer Chiu, Telluride Association Summer Program Scholarship Winner

Jennifer had the opportunity to experience college life while she was still in high school. As a junior at Hunter College High School in New York City, she won a full scholarship to the Telluride Association Summer Program on constitutional law at Cornell University. The program exposes students from a variety of backgrounds to college life and courses. Jennifer used her experience to make the transition to Yale University. In addition to this award, she also won the *New York Times* College Scholarship, National Merit Scholarship and Yale Club of New York City Scholarship. She gives the following advice about applying for awards, "Don't stress too much over sending in the perfect application. Behind every piece of paper is a person, not a robot."

Lessons from a Pitbull

Every time I walked down 52nd Avenue on my way home from the library, I passed a mean pitbull that always barked at and tried to attack strangers. For some reason, he seemed to hate me especially. I suppose that dogs instinctively protect their territory against all intruders and that I qualified. Yet, I was a very poor intruder at best. Whenever I saw him, I cowered next to the hedges, but he would always smell my fear and start his tirade. Perhaps it was my fault for not crossing over to the opposite sidewalk. I didn't want to admit to myself that I was scared.

One afternoon, after having had an especially bad day, I passed him once again. When he started to yap as usual, something snapped inside of me, and I growled back. I think that I could have been heard all the way into the next street. When the dog's owner came out to see what was going on, I ran away.

After that, I avoided the house.

On the surface, the conflict was simple: a struggle for territory. That dog simply did not want me around, while I insisted on it. But deeper down, the problem was my refusal to admit that I was scared of him. My foolish courage rested on the notion that I had a fear of being afraid. I refused to believe that every day is a struggle for survival, since humans have supposedly evolved beyond this. Obviously this is untrue, and now I realize that I, like any other creature, experience terror.

As I battled the dog, I felt conflict with myself at a deeper level. I realized I had a superiority complex, since I was better off in some ways than other people. That would boost my motivation to succeed, but it came at the cost of being alienated and eternally conscious of my weaknesses. I always watched my back, even when it was not necessary. I was intimidated by other people just like I was intimidated even by the dog. I paid the price of needless self-torture and confusion.

This barking episode was one decisive moment in my life. Though it is embarrassing, after all, I proved myself worthy against a dog, not all lessons can be picture-perfect. I'm glad I learned it the hard way than never at all. I realized that I am allowed to admit that I am afraid sometimes, as long as I am willing to work to mediate the anxiety.

Last week, I walked past the house again. It was abandoned and a "For Sale" sign adorned the front yard. I turned on my heels and left.

Essays about Family

Rodolfo Valadez, Cohen Foundation Scholarship Winner

Going to Thomas Jefferson High School in Los Angeles, California, Rodolfo discovered his passion: filmmaking. While making movies including his critically acclaimed documentary "los angeles," which was screened at the Sundance Film Festival, is his passion, Rodolfo's inspiration is his mother. Rodolfo freely admits that his mother is "my support, my help, my guidance, my friend, my hero." With this essay, Rodolfo won a $6,000 scholarship from the Cohen Foundation and $7,000 scholarship from the Hispanic Heritage Youth Awards to attend the University of California at Los Angeles.

A Mother's Sacrifice

My mother sat in between the dry grass growing out of the puddle of dirt water under a bridge in the hills separating Mexico from San Diego. In that exact moment I sat aboard a plane with strangers and in possession of a name other than mine in order to be granted admission into the United States. It has now been 14 years, and my mother still sacrifices her own comfort for mine. She works nine hours a day, six days a week in a machine-like position, humped over a sewing machine, altering clothes for strangers. At the same time I sit in class, socializing, enjoying a productive school day.

However, my mother is fulfilled knowing that her children take advantage of the vast opportunities this country has to offer despite the hardships she has to endure for a weekly paycheck. A paycheck she has vowed to invest into my college education at UCLA, an institution requiring almost $34,000 a year. At her hourly salary and after taxes she would have to work 2,560 hours in order to pay a year's tuition, which equals working 10,240 hours over the four years of college. If asked to, she would be more than willing to undergo the task of paying for my education knowing fully the standards and strife she would burden herself with.

In my sophomore year, I was among 24 honor students sequestered into a film course. I became one of the first students to attend the annual Telluride Film Festival in Colorado. In my second year in the course I attended the Sundance Film Festival where I was able to display my own work. Again, in my final year, we were invited to Sundance to show more films from our Academy of Film and Theatre Arts.

The film I showcased in the student forum was a documentary film commemorating my mother's struggle and sacrifice ever since her departure from a small oasis named Los Angeles in Durango, Mexico, only to move into the cold, industrial city of Los Angeles, California. The film depicts her struggle and reason for doing so. It also illuminates the fact that more like her exist all around us.

The film course at my high school has been my passion. For three years the course taught me to acquire a more perceptive and critical view of the world. Throughout the course we studied Aristotle's philosophies and the evolution of cinematography, and we analyzed films and wrote essays comparing the motifs they translate into a sequence of shots. I have become more creative and just recently started working on a new 16 mm film entitled "Love Story." As clichéd as the title suggests, the story is a satire of what the title represents. Such projects motivate me to work even when class is over. In the last three years I have found myself in class Saturday mornings and afternoons, editing and brainstorming ideas with classmates.

I have my mother to thank for being able to pursue my passion in filmmaking. I realize she gave up everything for me, and I will do what I can to make it well worth it.

Jessica Haskins, SuperCollege.com Scholarship Winner

Jessica's dream is to write fantasy novels and short stories. Throughout her time at Saratoga Springs High School in Saratoga Springs, New York, Jessica took challenging classes and focused on obtaining a wide breadth of knowledge that would be useful in her future career. She is studying creative writing at Bard College. Outside of classes, she keeps up her writing with day and dream journals. When writing her essay, Jessica had a difficult time with the length requirement. "Editing is terrible," she admits, but after much cutting she was able to pare down her essay to meet the requirements. Although Jessica was worried that her essay had lost much of its power, her editors assured her that it had not. Obviously, the judges concurred.

Thank You, Dr. Seuss

(With Special Recognition for the Trenton, Georgia, School System)

More than anything else I can think up as a reason, my mother is why I'm going to college. Because of her, there could be no other decision. Not that I'm being forced or anything, but she has heavily influenced me and my decision. In a good way.

She always regretted that she could never go to college. Her parents, her teachers and her school counselors somehow, even though I still have trouble understanding it, simply never arranged it for her. College has always been a foregone conclusion for me, so this seems bizarre. To this day, she's never been able to explain it to my satisfaction. Nor to her own.

My mother is a very intelligent woman and was one of the best students in her small-town, athletics-minded Georgia high school (3rd or so in her class, where rank was unweighted and the valedictorian did as little as she could to get 100's in easy classes). She's certain that she could have accomplished a lot in life if she'd only been able to get a college education. She swears her education actually stopped at 9th grade, when she moved from Illinois to Georgia. I've seen the white sticker she uses as a bookmark in her gigantic Random House Dictionary of the English Language. It says "I [heart] Georgia," with the heart crossed out in black marker. She does love things like warm weather, big flowers and Southern cooking but despises their educational system.

I grew up knowing how keenly she lamented her missed opportunity, and she passed on her appreciation for the value of education to me. From the start she raised me to be an intellectual. I could read by age 3. I have a vivid memory of lying on the couch with her in the living room of our old house right on Route 9, where the cars would streak past day and night. My mother was reading Dr. Seuss to me—"We run for fun in the hot, hot sun," from *One Fish, Two Fish, Red Fish, Blue Fish*—and afternoon sunlight was pouring in through the windows, warming the whole room. As she read, I followed along. That was my first memory of ever actually reading the words, rather than just being read to. Whenever I think of my educational success, I attribute it first and foremost to learning to read at an early age, and the very next thing I think of is that reading lesson in the sun.

I have another memory. Me, at about the same age, confronting my father in the bathroom and asking, "Daddy, when can I go to school?" I just couldn't wait. I went to two years of preschool, where I did very well, except that I wasn't very generous. Recently I was poking through my old school files and found a couple of reports from one of my preschools. In fact, let me go get them so that I can quote it exactly—ah, here it is. "Jessica needs prompting to share." I found that very amusing. Now that I think about it, I was pretty attached to that Viewmaster.

When I was finally old enough I went to kindergarten, but nothing there was a challenge for me, and my parents and I all wanted me to skip a grade. It took a little battling with the school, which was reluctant to move me ahead, and some extensive testing, but they finally agreed to have me skip first grade. I'm glad that I did. Even though I was younger than the other kids in my grade, I took advanced classes whenever there was an opportunity. Because of the importance my mother always placed on education, I was always ready to take on harder material.

As I said before, it was always a given that I would go to college. My mother wanted it for me, and I wanted it for myself. And not just any college—my aim was never to just get a degree and a good job, but to continue to enrich myself. The "good job" isn't even guaranteed. After all, I want to be a writer, and there's no ticket to success in that field without a good bit of luck. So my standards for college are slightly different. Basically what I want is the most liberal of liberal arts. I want to continue the educational path that started way back when I was lying on the living room couch reading *One Fish, Two Fish, Red Fish, Blue Fish* with my mother, who knew I'd someday get the college experience she never had. So thank you, Dr. Seuss. And thank you, Mom.

The Intangible Benefits of Applying
U.C. Berkeley Scholarship Connection

You have something to gain by applying for scholarships even if you don't win says Leah Carroll, coordinator of U.C. Berkeley's Haas Scholars program and former program coordinator of the university's Scholarship Connection. In her roles Carroll has assisted Berkeley students with applying for awards, especially for the highly competitive scholarships, including the Rhodes, Marshall and Truman.

While Carroll gives students feedback on their essays and practices interviewing them, she reminds them that there is more than scholarship dollars at stake.

"I also emphasize the fringe benefits. For starters you get to know your professors better than before since you need to speak with them," she says. Carroll adds, "You also get practice presenting yourself in interviews and on paper." This is helpful for students who will soon be applying for jobs or for graduate school. She says that the essays can even serve as rough drafts of graduate school admission essays.

And looking at the big picture, Carroll says that applying for one of these awards "forces you to analyze your own life." She says that one of the things she enjoys most about her job is helping students clarify their purpose in life through the process of applying for scholarships.

Donald H. Matsuda, Jr., Truman Scholarship Winner

Working as an intern for a health clinic, Donald read an article in the *New York Times.* The headline was, "Forty-four Million Americans without Health Insurance." When he learned through the article that over one-third of these Americans were children, he decided to take action. With the help of the clinic's director, he secured the funding for and developed a series of insurance drives for Asian immigrant children. In addition to his work with the clinic, Donald is the founder of the San Mateo Children's Health Insurance Program, the national director of United Students for Veterans' Health and the founder of the Nepal Pediatric Clinical Internship.

A Stanford University student from Sacramento, California, where he attended Jesuit High School, Donald plans to use the $30,000 Truman Scholarship to obtain a medical degree and master's degree in public administration and would eventually like to be the medical director of a nonprofit clinic to aid underserved populations and the uninsured.

When Drinking Water

When drinking water, my grandmother would often proclaim, "Never forget its source." For some reason, I always enjoyed hearing her repeat these words of wisdom from her book of ancient Asian proverbs. Perhaps it was because I had grown to fully appreciate its true meaning—that one must always remember and treasure their ancestry and elders, who are viewed as the ultimate source of life. Or, perhaps it was because I felt this proverb effectively expressed my own sentiments about my life.

Growing up as an only child, I developed a very close relationship with my entire family and I greatly valued the time I was able to spend in the company of my elders, especially my grandmother. As a survivor of the Japanese American internment camps, she maintained an unbridled idealism, an impeccable work ethic and a genuine compassion for those in need. Moreover, she was intent on instilling these values in me when I was a young boy. I often looked to her as my true source of strength, for she always infused me with energy, passion and ideals.

Two years ago, I received a call from my parents urging me to return home. When I got there, I saw my mother was on the verge of tears as she told me what was wrong: "Grandma passed away today. She had a massive stroke and the doctors did everything they could, but..." I embraced my mother and we cried for what seemed like an eternity. I soon realized that I had lost not only my grandmother, but also a precious source of inspiration and strength.

Since that tragic day, I have become a much stronger person. I have internalized grandma's work ethic, idealism and compassion so that my source of strength now comes from within. It is this new motivation that fuels my convictions and drives my passion for a life dedicated to public service.

Every day, when I pass by the elegantly sculpted water fountains on my way to class, I pause as cherished memories of my grandmother fill my mind, and I know in my heart that I will never forget my true source.

Essay Advice from the Winners
Scholarship Winners

Here are some essay tips from scholarship winners. Having survived various competitions these winners have a unique understanding of what goes into crafting a winning essay.— Gen & Kelly

Sara Bei
Stanford University student and scholarship winner
"Sometimes the ones you end up winning are the ones you almost didn't apply for. Even if it takes a long time to fill out applications and write essays, think of it as being paid $500 an hour if you win."

Jason Morimoto
U.C. Berkeley student and scholarship winner
"Use your essay to craft a story showing why you are a unique candidate. Include personal experiences, lessons learned and how you are trying to improve yourself."

Chheng Sok, Chicago Scholars Foundation Winner

Every time Chheng announced good news to her parents, they gave her their special smile. Her parents grew up in Cambodia, where her father's education ended in grade school and her mother did not receive a formal education. So it held special meaning when Chheng was accepted to the University of Chicago. She received her parents' special smile. And when she won more than $35,000 in scholarships, their smile broadened even wider.

Graduating from Lane Technical School in Chicago, Chheng was president of the Chinese Club and involved in public service. She encourages others to apply for scholarships. As she says, "I'm not exactly the best student, but I still got scholarships." Majoring in East Asian Language and Civilization and Economics at the University of Chicago, she plans a career in education or international business.

My Family's Hope

My family and I immigrated to the United States from Cambodia to flee the ravages of the Khmer Rouge when I was only a year old. We did not have a single penny when we came to the United States. I remember seeing my father diligently collect soda cans on the streets to trade in to the local recycling center for a penny each. I remember watching my family silently endure the rudeness of waiters and salespeople because we did not speak grammatically correct English and realizing at the age of five how much illiteracy paralyzes a person.

I am the youngest out of my parent's nine children, yet I possess the greatest amount of education. My father can barely read English. My mother is totally illiterate. Due to my family's financial situation, none of my eight siblings have completed college. Throughout my elementary and high school years, I oftentimes had difficulty with my schoolwork. I remember staying up late at night, sometimes until two in the morning, just so that I could figure out the answer to a homework problem. My parents and older siblings, as much as they wanted to help me on my assignments, were unable to because they simply did not understand the material. They would quietly sit by me and bring me refreshments from time to time and offer me encouragement. My siblings make me realize how priceless knowledge is and to make the most out of one's education.

My parents look at me as my family's hope for the future. They dream that I will some day graduate from an American university. They want to be able to send back letters to our relatives in China and in Cambodia, telling them about how one person in the family has gained an American diploma. I want to be the realization of their dream and my dream. I dream of graduating from one of the finest colleges in America, the University of Chicago. I hope that someday I will be able to repay my parents for all the years they have lovingly supported me. I want to be able to financially and intellectually provide for my family so that we no longer have to endure the discrimination toward illiteracy.

In addition, I strive to succeed in school because I want to be a role model for my nieces and nephews. As a student, I personally know how tough it can be to excel in school. I want to be there to help them if they need help on a class assignment, to guide them through their first multiplication table and to be their mentor when they start the college selection process.

With knowledge, one need not fear being cheated by a salesman or being looked down upon by an egotistical snob. Education is the door that opens the path to knowledge. With knowledge, I am in control of my life and my destiny.

Essay Advice from the Winners
Scholarship Winners

Here are some essay tips from scholarship winners. Having survived various competitions these winners have a unique understanding of what goes into crafting a winning essay.— Gen & Kelly

Donald H. Matsuda, Jr.
Stanford University student and Truman Scholar
"If readers can connect with you, feel your emotions and feel they know you, that you're such a dynamic person, that comes across in your writing. That really is a plus. You can espouse all the pros and cons of think tanks in the American political system but that doesn't really help the committee learn who you are."

Dalia Alcázar
U.C. Berkeley student and scholarship winner
"Your essays are the most time consuming part of applying. Some of the questions are very similar. You might have a couple essays already written that you can modify. For many of the scholarships I won I used the same essay with slight modifications."

Jessica Haskins
Bard College student and scholarship winner
"The topic doesn't have to be profound. You don't have to write about the time you saved someone's life, or describe an earth-shattering experience—I personally think that a simple, thoughtful and honest reflection carries more weight than an elevated epic of love, loss and life's lessons in 500 words or less."

Alex Dao, Gates Millennium Scholarship

A student at Stanford University, Alex won several scholarships including the Maria Hart Becker Scholarship Fund, Sam Walton Scholarship and Robert C. Byrd Scholarship. He says he didn't expect to win all of the scholarships that he did and advises students, "If you don't apply, you'll never win. Let the scholarship judges know who you really are."

Childhood

Every time I open up our photo albums during Christmas and family gatherings I feel a sense of nostalgia. With each turn of the page, each resonance of laughter, each event and each year—precisely remembered—all the problems of today vanish: my parents never divorced, my father never lost his job and my family never moved. Instead, life is filled with memories of happy and exuberant times. Although those days are now rooted far in the past, the memories of life as a child stay vivid and clear.

Life had always been carefree and pleasant. I had cousins who loved me, parents who disciplined me and girls who teased me. I felt all the warmth and comfort any child could want; however, it was more than just this that made my childhood "perfect." I had always been close to my brothers, and the most memorable moments of my childhood embrace the love and affection my brothers and I shared. We spent countless summer days playing and dreaming on the front lawn. We wrestled and fought, imitating those we saw on television. Yet, with our short attention spans, it wasn't long before we sat down together and started talking about our hopes for the future, our ambitions and goals, our future wives and children. Innocently, I had always thought becoming a superhero was a realistic goal. I talked about all the superpowers I would somehow acquire and how people would tell stories of my accomplishments for generations to come. My brothers, although younger, laughed and made fun; after all, they had more realistic ambitions, hoping to become doctors or lawyers. Then the debates began. We went on and on for hours, talking about how each of us would be better than the others. Although I did not always claim first place, I looked forward to the next day when we'd come back out and start our discussions anew. As simple as it may seem, their presence was more than enough to make me happy. These experiences understandably may not seem like much to an outside observer, but for me they are among the best days of my life. To this day I can still think of no better way I could have spent my summer days than just sitting in the front yard, enjoying the company of my siblings. Nothing even comes close.

Although it's been many years since then, I have always longed to return to this past: every day was an experience in its own and filled with nothing but excitement and joy. As I look back on my childhood, I contemplate the things that made it so enjoyable—the simplicity of life as a child. I was devoid of responsibilities, satisfied with life and hopeful for the future. My childhood was instrumental in shaping who I have become: someone driven to succeed but optimistic even in the face of failure. Through years past, I have realized that life will never be the same, but then again, when does life ever stay the same? Each day presents a new set of problems. I can no longer just sit in the front yard with my brothers, dreaming the day away. Instead, I must confront these challenges and do my best to resolve them. Although times have changed and obstacles have arisen, I still view the future with the same optimism and anticipation I have always viewed it with. My experiences have hardly been "perfect," but life continues to amaze and excite me at every turn. The problems of "yesterday" should not affect the futures of "tomorrow."

National or International Issues

Elizabeth Ashlea Wood, Optimist International Essay Contest Winner

After having witnessed a nuclear disaster, Elizabeth knew that her life was changed. She says, "It really opened my eyes. It got me away from thinking that I'm young and can live forever." Touched, she wrote about the experience for this award to share her fear and realizations with others. A graduate of the Classen School of Advanced Studies for Performing and Visual Arts in Oklahoma City, she is studying literature, writing and the arts at Eugene Lang College in New York City.

The Tokai Nuclear Disaster

Last year on an October evening in Japan, I enjoyed the rain, walking slowly to my host family's farm for the night. After I yelled the customary "Tadaima" and removed my shoes my host mother pulled out a heavy English dictionary. She searched for a word and then pointed excitedly. Above her finger I read "radiation." The Tokai nuclear power plant two miles away was experiencing a severe accident. Soon trucks driving by screamed warnings in Japanese to prepare for nuclear disaster. My body was numb.

I had been to Hiroshima the week before. All I could imagine were the grotesque pictures of goiters and dripping flesh. Photographs of the burnt remains of an ancient city flashed in my head. I remembered seeing the "Daisy Girl" commercial from LBJ's presidential campaign in government class. It slowly played in my mind, a blonde child holding a daisy, framed by a green-gray mushroom cloud. My imagination forced me to expect the worst.

The air terrified me. I thought I was suffocating. In that moment I could not understand how my life had led to this crucial moment. I had left my home for a beautiful opportunity to live in Japan and experience the culture. I had joined an exchange program in a small village by the ocean. This succession of serendipitous events led me to the only place in the entire world where a severe nuclear disaster was occurring. My choices had exposed me to the ultimate weapon of our time; I was waiting for radiation to subside. The rice paper windows and layers of silk robes provided little comfort. There was nothing I could do to protect myself from the danger. In that moment I could only learn.

The world's issues no longer can disappear as I close a schoolbook. On that autumn evening I was suddenly a part of one of the nemeses of the twentieth century: nuclear energy. Ironically, my frightening experience was only an accident. When I decided to embrace a three-month adventure I never expected to trade in theater and friends for a serious nuclear disaster. My eyes were pried open to make me realize that the world's issues are not separate from my American life. I realized that I had been educated about the world to understand cause and effects, the cycles of history and of the future, but I had not metacognitively incorporated them into a worldview.

That evening reached into my mind and opened a door to the realities of this world. The Tokai disaster threatened my life, but it also demonstrated the capabilities for any person to experience the same shocking circumstances. In Japan, quarantined for days on a Buddhist farm, I could see no separation of myself from other cultures. I realized that I could no longer segregate America from other countries, my race from other races, Oklahoma from Japan. Three days after the Tokai nuclear disaster I stepped out of the farmhouse into the fresh sunshine of a glorious oriental garden. Over a cup of green tea I determined to be committed to my new perception of the world as an entirety.

Elisa Tatiana Juárez, Target All-Around Scholarship Winner

Based on her research in osteoporosis and gerontology, Elisa has placed first and best in show in a number of science competitions including the Intel International Science and Engineering Fair and the South Florida Science and Engineering Fair. But each time she entered a science competition, she noticed that economically disadvantaged students were underrepresented. She did something to change this. Working with the Miami Museum of Science and Big Brothers Big Sisters of Greater Miami, she founded the Students and Teachers Advocating Research Science (STARS) program to provide assistance to economically-disadvantaged middle school children.

In addition to STARS, Elisa has been recognized by the United States Air Force for her research in gerontology and was selected to present her work to the Florida state legislature for her research on osteoporosis. Her commitment to the sciences has paid off. She has won scholarships including the National Hispanic Heritage Youth Award for Science and Technology and the Science Silver Knight Award. A graduate of Coral Reef Senior High School in Miami, she is a student at Brown University.

STARS

I developed the STARS (Students and Teachers Advocating Research Science) Project to provide information, materials and, most importantly, mentors to help middle school students from at-risk environments to complete and present successful science projects. STARS now helps the Miami Museum of Science and Big Brothers Big Sisters of Greater Miami to "support and empower single-parent families to actively engage in their children's science education."

STARS grew as an extension of my own involvement with science research projects that have been successful at local, regional, state and international levels. I had a lot of support from family, teachers and mentors and wanted to find a way to offer similar support and opportunities for students who didn't have all that. American students are losing ground internationally in science and math, and I wanted to find a way to share my passion in tangible ways.

Why science? I feel that it is important for every kid to be involved in science. The Third International Mathematics and Science Study (TIMSS) showed that U.S. 12th graders outperformed only two (Cyprus and South Africa) of the 21 participating countries in math and science. All kids need to have access to better opportunities in science, and this project has allowed kids who had never even thought about science research to discover that they can do anything they want to do.

I think the most memorable part of this project was to see the kids' eyes sparkle when they talked about their ideas for projects and then began to see the results of actually doing the research. I remember at the end of a workshop, one of the girls came up to me and said that she really enjoyed the day. I asked her what she meant, and she said with a smile, "Well, I don't really do science. I'm more into English and literature. When I heard about this, I didn't really want to come, but I am so glad I did. I had so much fun learning that I could do a good project. I think my teacher will be proud."

I am now designing a STARS science curriculum that correlates with the National Science Education Standards. I hope that Big Brothers Big Sisters chapters around the country will be able to use the curriculum to encourage their "littles" and "bigs" to participate more actively in science.

Based on this experience so far, I would tell other young people that there is nothing more rewarding than realizing that you can make a difference. That you can identify a need, develop a solution, find people to help you accomplish your goals. Of course, I would also tell them that science is everywhere and is exciting and can help you learn about the universe and about yourself.

Elisa Tatiana Juárez, Presbyterian Church USA Scholarship Winner

The Power to Change the World

When people ask me what I want to do when I grow up, I answer them quite simply and firmly, "I am going to change the world." I am 17 years old, but I have known for a very long time that I would, in some way, be responsible for shaping the world of the future. Crazy? Maybe. Impossible? Definitely not.

Unfortunately, in my experience, it has been kids my age who tell me that I am just a dreamer and that there is no way I could possibly make a difference in the world. "Come on Elisa," they tell me, "You're just a kid. No one in his or her right mind is going to listen to some high school girl. Don't bother; no one cares anyway. Someone else will do it."

I think that the greatest opportunity facing youth today is the power to better the world around us by using new tools, new technologies and a new understanding of the global community. By the same token I believe that the most urgent problem facing youth today is indifference. The general attitude about everything and anything is "Who cares? I am not that important, there is nothing I can do about it." I find this incredibly sad and distressing. God gives us the intelligence to build the tools; we only need to use them with the guidance of His Spirit guided by His love.

My generation is very cynical when it comes to helping out. They claim that what they have to say couldn't possibly be important enough to be heard by others. What they don't understand are two very important concepts. First of all, the majority of the youth today don't realize that there are plenty of problems in their own community. Making a difference doesn't always mean moving to Somalia to end hunger. It could mean something along the lines of helping a migrant family learn the basics of the English language. Second of all, youth today don't realize how something very simple can change someone's entire world. By teaching that family English, for example, they will feel more comfortable in this country.

Growing up I heard a story about an old man who goes down to the sea one morning. He notices that a young girl is reaching down and throwing starfish into the water. Curious, he walks over to the girl and asks her what she is doing. She replies, "Well, the tide is awfully low, and if I don't throw the starfish into the water the sun will dry them out." The old man looked at her and laughed. There were miles of shore with thousands of starfish. The little girl couldn't possibly throw all the starfish back in the sea. He told her she wouldn't be able to make a difference. The little girl bent down scooping up yet another starfish. She turned it over in her hand processing what the man had told her. Then, looking at the old man, she placed the starfish in his hands and helped him throw it back into the sea and moved on to the next starfish. She looked over her shoulder and said, "Well, to that starfish, I made a world of difference."

This is where the story traditionally ends. I have added on to it. The man, realizing the power this little girl had over the lives of the starfish, called up his grandchildren. Together they worked at saving the stranded starfish. That day, maybe not all the starfish were saved, but those that were, I'm sure, were very grateful. They continued living because of the determination of a little girl who knew that she could make a difference and could find ways to get others involved.

We must each find our starfish. If we throw our stars wisely and well, the world will be blessed. I constantly am praying for the strength to carry on and for the courage to help others find the power within them to help shape the world of today.

Shashank Bengali, Scripps-Howard College Journalism Scholarship Winner

Shashank knew that his parents wouldn't be able to foot the entire bill for his education at a private college, especially since his younger brother would soon follow him to college. Rather than look for a less-expensive school, Shashank decided to take action by applying for scholarships. His advisers at Whitney High School in Cerritos, California, suggested that he apply for the awards for which he would be the best candidate. Journalism awards were a natural fit.

Since the age of 13, Shashank has worked for his school newspaper. As the editor, he won a national competition for the Knight Ridder Minority Journalism Scholarship, which allowed him to intern at four newspapers across the country while in school. In addition, he won a full-tuition scholarship from the University of Southern California and Scripps-Howard College Journalism Scholarship, awarded to 10 college journalists in the country. He recently graduated with a degree in broadcast journalism, political science and French and is working as a Missouri state correspondent for *The Kansas City Star.*

Media Misunderstandings

On the day of the New Hampshire primary this year, the online magazine Slate.com posted early exit-poll results on its site before voting had closed for the day, inciting an enormous outcry in the traditional media. The major newspapers and television networks, bound by contract to honor an embargo on those results, said Slate violated the law—and a journalistic trust with the people. Slate disagreed, and went ahead publishing exit-poll results on the days of several other primaries this season, before being threatened with a lawsuit.

On the question of law, at least, Slate never agreed to any embargo. The other question, of the people's trust, is murkier, because it's unclear whether knowing preliminary election results actually deters voters from going to the polls. Tempers ran high on both sides here, with Slate columnist Jack Schafer going so far as to write in a *Wall Street Journal* op-ed piece that the Big Three networks' coverage of primary results is "all an act."

I bring up this story to illustrate a point: the relationship between "old" and "new" media is in real disrepair. Finger-pointing and mutual misunderstanding rule the day, when diverse news organizations hardly seem, most times, to understand each other's roles. The fact is, there are now three ways to disseminate information in the world—in print, in broadcast and online. All three have merit, and all three, in some form or another, appear to be here to stay.

What's needed, then, is greater cooperation and less co-optation. If, as many believe, the best news organizations of the near future will be those that are diversified and bring elements of print, broadcast and online media to bear together on their coverage, those journalists who are trained in each form will be the most valuable. I subscribe to this view and I will be one of those "hybrid" journalists, helping guide a shift to more complete, convergent news coverage that encompasses the three forms because I know the power of each.

I consider myself lucky to be around for the old media-new media debate because it's a vital one. I believe that much of the disdain on both sides is a product of misconceptions—and a lack of experience. My generation's position is unique: I've grown up with 24-hour news channels and the Internet, so I know their immediacy and reach in a visceral way. But the reason I got into journalism in the first place was that I love the written word and the prudence of print media. I know that people will always need their daily newspaper and their weekly newsmagazine, no matter how quickly TV and websites can give them their fix.

So I've explored all three realms of journalism during my time in college, and I've discovered that I'm a journalist first and foremost, gladly unfettered by any other labels. Internships at newspapers have reinforced my newsgathering and writing skills. My time as executive producer of USC's nightly newscast has taught me that "print values" can be tuned for broadcast—for visual impact and swift, assured responses to breaking-news situations. And each time a distant friend or relative e-mails me to say they saw our webcast and have feedback, or (better yet) to offer story ideas from their part of the world, I learn the power of the Internet as a medium of news.

Good journalism can be done with these three modes working in concert, but the best journalism can only come with responsible and well-trained leaders at the top, who know how to direct multifaceted coverage because they believe in it and have done it before. That's what I want to do and am learning how to do—help lead the new wave.

I would encourage the sort of synergy that Tribune is pursuing—and that reporters at CNN practice daily when they submit their stories for that network's TV, radio and online products. There is no reason consumers shouldn't have the benefit of the fullest possible picture in a news story; after all, it's what we should strive to give them each time around. Already, on a small scale, I am working to achieve that convergence on our campus. Next year, our newscast and the student newspaper—two entirely distinct organizations—will team up for one in-depth story. We will each pursue the angles to that story that are best suited to our particular medium—visual stories for TV, for example, and longer analysis pieces for print—and we'll use our websites to complete the coverage, including any long documents or transcripts of interviews that can't fit newshole or airtime.

A news organization should be dedicated to the kind of public service in journalism that may uproot the company's tradition for the sake of its work. It makes good business sense, because through responsible convergence you can reach more people with greater speed than your competition. But most important, it improves the product—and that is good journalism.

Of course, I don't know exactly how I'm going to get to a position where I can help implement this vision I share. One thing that's certain about this changing market is that nothing's certain. For the time being, after graduating college, I plan to write for a newspaper—because that's my first love, and still the traditional journalist's ground zero. That's a personal bias, I admit, but my experience in the other realms will probably make me a better print reporter. From that first job to wherever I end up, it's a yet-to-be-paved road. But I am confident in the future of journalism in this new era, and I'll remain dedicated to it.

Lindsay Hyde, National React Take Action Award & Toyota Scholar Winner

When her grandmother received a corneal transplant that saved her vision, it motivated Lindsay to ensure that others were educated about the benefits of organ donation. From this single experience the Organ Donor Project was born.

Over three years, the Miami student secured corporate sponsorships to produce an educational curriculum and informational video for other students to view and create their own organ donation awareness programs. The project expanded from Lindsay's own high school, Southwest Miami High School, to 12 schools across the nation and five in Malaysia, Australia, Costa Rica and the United Kingdom.

The Importance of Getting Editors
Donald H. Matsuda, Jr., Truman Scholar

The Truman Scholarship competition requires that each applicant write a detailed policy statement. This is a rigorous academic paper about a topic of national or international importance. However, there is nothing that says you cannot seek help. In fact, we recommend that regardless of your essay topic—whether a policy statement or personal narrative—you find others to read the essay and provide constructive feedback.

Donald maximized the knowledge of the people around him when writing his essay. He says, "I obtained advice from at least 10 different people, professors, experts in health care policy, the director of fellowships, my honors research advisor, a number of other Stanford students who had won Trumans in the past, friends and parents."

In fact, Donald credits his win to the many people who helped. He says, "It's a long process and requires quite a bit of emotional reflection. I really am indebted to them. I don't think I could have been successful without their help."

As a result of her efforts, Lindsay won a number of scholarships including being a National Coca-Cola Scholar, National Toyota Scholar and National React Take Action Award winner. At Harvard University, she is studying sociology and women's studies as well as continuing her volunteer work as the founder of Strong Women, Strong Girls, designed to assist at-risk elementary school girls.

Organ Donor Project

Imagine a stadium filled with 100,000 football fans. The stadium would overflow with people, the sound of cheering would be deafening. Now, imagine the game has finished, but the fans are unable to leave. Instead they sit waiting, waiting for...the unknown. By next year, experts estimate that 100,000 people will be waiting for life-saving organ transplants.

For several months, my grandmother was a fan in that stadium, waiting for a sight-saving corneal transplant. My grandmother was fortunate to receive her transplant, thanks to the generosity of individuals who made the decision to become organ donors.

As a result of my grandmother's experience, I realized the importance of organ donation and the need for accurate organ donation education. To meet this need, I developed a community service project during my sophomore year to provide teenagers with accurate organ donation information. The Organ Donor Project was introduced with a three-day awareness event that included a pep rally, speakers day and fundraising paintball tournament. Over 700 teachers and students participated in these awareness activities, 400 of which made the decision to become organ donors. As project founder, I procured over $5,000 in prize giveaway and in-kind donations, secured community support and coordinated the three-day event. That same year, the Organ Donor Project was recognized at the International Community Problem Solving Forum for its outstanding service to the Dade County community with a first place international award.

The second year of the Organ Donor Project brought tremendous growth. As a part of my efforts to increase teen awareness of the myths and misconceptions surrounding organ donation, I scripted an informational "Fact or Fiction" video. To make this video a reality, I secured the $10,000 in production costs from Burger King Corporation. The video received a

Special Achievement Award from the Miami Children's Film Festival for its outstanding educational value.

Also in the second year of the Organ Donor Project, I authored a step-by-step workbook designed to guide teenagers through the process of creating an organ donation awareness project. Recognizing the value of the student workbook, Hoffman-La Roche Laboratories underwrote its publication. This workbook is currently being utilized by the Transplant Foundation of South Florida in Dade, Broward, Palm Beach and Monroe counties as a part of its educational outreach efforts.

In response to the outpouring of enthusiasm demonstrated for the Project by educators at my school, I realized that classroom curriculum would serve as a means of educating young people of the need for organ donation. Using the Sunshine State Standards for Education as a guide, I wrote interdisciplinary organ donation curriculum for grades 3 to 12. This curriculum was utilized by teachers at Southwest High, Riviera Middle and Cypress Elementary schools. The curriculum was recognized in a national contest by Co-NECT, Inc. for its outstanding community value.

Now in its third year, the Organ Donor Project has expanded into 17 schools nationally and internationally, through a partnership with the Interact Service Club. As project founder, I am coordinating the efforts of students at Southwest High School serving as "e-bassadors" to schools in the United States, Malaysia, Australia, Ireland, Costa Rica and Panama. Utilizing Internet resources and communication, the students are exchanging information and ideas for organ donation education activities. The schools involved are utilizing the Organ Donor Project Student Workbook, "Fact or Fiction" video and interdisciplinary curriculum to increase awareness of the need for organ donation in their communities. The final product of this collaboration will be the creation of an International Organ Donation Information Exchange that will explore the cultural, legal and ethical implications of organ donation internationally. Through the efforts of the Organ Donor Project, thousands of teens have become aware of the desperate need for organ donation.

Community Service & Volunteerism

Vanessa Deanne Perplies, Target All-Around Scholarship Winner

As a volunteer for the Los Angeles Police Department Explorer Scout Program, Vanessa has assisted with crime prevention surveillance, evidence searches and police ride alongs. She volunteered nearly 400 hours with the program designed for students who are interested in law enforcement and community service. Her work was one of the reasons she won the Target All-Around Scholarship, which is based on community service. In addition to volunteering with the Explorer Scout Program, Vanessa also raised funds and walked with the North Hollywood High School Zoo Magnet AIDS team and volunteered for Project Chicken Soup preparing and delivering food to AIDS patients. A student at U.C. Santa Barbara, she is majoring in sociology and plans to become either a sociologist or journalist.

Serving & Protecting

One Sunday morning, bright and early, approximately 25 Girl Scouts arrived for a tour of the Los Angeles Police Department Foothill Police Station.

As a Los Angeles Police Department Explorer Scout, it was my task to help these girls. Experiences like this one have shaped and solidified my career goals, in addition to benefiting the children of Los Angeles.

The girls, ranging in ages from 4 to 11, had not only an enjoyable adventure but also learned about important issues such as 911, acting in emergencies and overall safety. I helped the girls try on riot gear, turn on the lights and sirens of police cars and use the police radios. I escorted them through empty jail cells, reminding them of the dangers of the world and teaching them to stay safe.

For young girls who are rarely taught self-reliance, this experience taught them how to take care of themselves. I was keeping people safe as well as helping them grow up to be stronger, wiser women. I could see their delight and curiosity at the unfamiliar environment of a police station, and I was happy to demystify law enforcement in such a positive manner.

The gratitude of the little girls showed me the simple appreciation in a child's smile was a priceless feeling. The Girl Scouts were not the only ones who learned; I realized that the things that make me happiest also make others happy. I have been inspired and challenged to learn and do more, and especially to reach out and share the knowledge I can, changing the lives of others for the better.

More Essay Advice from the Winners
Scholarship Winners

Here are some more tips on crafting your essay from scholarship winners.—Gen & Kelly

Jason Morimoto
U.C. Berkeley student and scholarship winner
"The way to shine is by crafting a story in your essay that brings out your strengths. I like to give a lot of personal examples as to why I am involved in certain activities. I try to avoid the generic responses like 'it was a good learning experience' or 'I wanted to try something new.' For example, I often use the example of how I walked on to a national champion rugby team as a mere 5'6" player with no prior experience. The coach took one look at me and wanted to laugh. I told him that all I wanted was a tryout. With a lot of determination and hard work, I proved myself capable of playing with world class athletes."

Kristin N. Javaras
Rhodes Scholar
"I highly recommend showing it to people who have won fellowships themselves or who have read successful fellowship application essays before (and the more people the better). Also, I feel that the revision process was crucial for my essay: I went through about seven or eight drafts of my personal statement!"

Svati Singla, Discover Card Tribute Award Scholarship Winner

Svati says that she has never let society's perception of age stop her. This was one of the factors that led her to publish an abstract in the American Journal of Hypertension after years of research–at the age of 11. Throughout junior high and high school, she continued her research at East Carolina University on fetal alcohol syndrome, won accolades from the U.S. Navy and Army for her research and spent three years shadowing surgeons at East Carolina University Health Systems.

After graduating from J.H. Rose High School in Greenville, North Carolina, Svati is studying biology with a concentration in genetics at Duke University. She has won an extraordinary $1 million in scholarships including the Discover Card Gold Tribute Award, Benjamin N. Duke Leadership Scholarship, Boy Scouts of America National Scholarship and National Merit Scholarship. After graduating, she plans to attend medical school.

Giving Back to My Community

I dedicate many hours of my time to significant community service activities. Through my participation in such service projects and activities, I have learned many valuable lessons about the significance of each individual in the community.

As a literacy volunteer, I am given the opportunity to see the glow on a mother's face when she realizes that her son will finally be given the gift of the ability to read. I am given the satisfaction of knowing that my time is positively contributing to another's life.

Another community service activity that has significantly influenced the community is my involvement in Teen Court. Teen Court is an alternative program to the court system that provides graduated penalties for juvenile offenders. It is an innovative program that benefits teens on both sides of the court system. The teens who are brought before the Teen Court learn to accept the consequences of their actions, without having a flaw in their permanent record. On the other hand, the teens that comprise the court system are educated about the justice system while they work together for awareness and compliance with the law. As a member of the Teen Court program, I am able to provide far-reaching benefits for all members of the community by keeping the youth well disciplined and well educated.

Recognizing the need for volunteers at a facility for mentally retarded children, I immediately seized the opportunity to make a difference in the lives of these children. As I read and play with them, I realize how simple pleasures bring so much satisfaction and joy to their hearts. I take great pride, knowing that I am spreading a feeling of warmth and happiness with my actions. At the local Boy's and Girl's Club, I have initiated a program, called "Bookworm", which encourages young children to read. As I go and read to these children, I realize that I am not only increasing their interest in reading, but that I am also serving as a role model to them. The children are all motivated to learn and make great strides in their reading. Their interest in education creates a positive attitude towards learning that is beneficial to the community.

As I volunteer for other organizations such as the Salvation Army, American Cancer Society, Knights of Columbus, Greenville Community Shelter, East Carolina University Health Systems and more, I realize how my actions can be compared to a pebble in a pond. Despite the size of the pebble, once it is thrown into the pond, the entire pond feels the pebble's impact through the ripples. Similarly, though I am just one individual in a large community, I am able to make a difference. Dedicated to community service, I am the pebble in the pond.

Donald H. Matsuda, Jr., Truman Scholarship Winner

Camp ReCreation

Working with mentally and physically disabled children over the past four summers has been one of the most amazing and rewarding experiences of my undergraduate career. Before volunteering with Camp ReCreation for Disabled Kids, I shied away from any interaction with the disabled community and remained distant from this group of people whose lives and problems seemed so very different from my own. Nevertheless, I felt compelled to bridge this gap, and I decided to board the bus for my first experience at Camp ReCreation.

During this first summer, I took care of a deaf boy named Michael. At first, I was quite frustrated because I was unable to establish any means of communication with him. However, I did not see this problem as an insurmountable obstacle; instead, I viewed it as a challenge that could be overcome with some dedication and perseverance on my part. Over the next week, I voraciously read all books I could find on sign language, and I devoted most of my nights to mastering this very complex form of communication. My tireless efforts paid off, as Michael began to recognize my signs and responded with frequent smiles, indicating his understanding and acceptance. As Michael began to open up and even sign back, I realized that we had developed a special and meaningful relationship—one that provided him with happiness and one that solidified my genuine love of service.

I eagerly returned to camp for three more summers. One summer I worked with Nick, a mildly autistic teenager to improve his communication skills. Last year, I helped Brittney, a young girl with a neurological disorder, in developing better motor coordination. Despite the differing needs of each camper, I still maintained the camp's mission: to provide a positive and healthy summer experience for disabled youth. In return, I gained the love and friendship of disabled kids and learned that these children have needs that are not unlike my own. I truly value my Camp ReCreation experience because it has fueled my passion to protect and promote the rights of children nationwide.

Emily Kendall, Association for Women in Science Scholarship Winner

To tutor a struggling math student, Emily drew on the patience that her own teachers had shown her when she was younger. This is the topic of Emily's essay, which she wrote to win a number of scholarships and to apply to Harvard, Duke, MIT, Washington University in St. Louis, Caltech, Vanderbilt and the University of Chicago. In fact, she not only gained admission to all but also received a number of offers of full scholarships. In addition to her volunteer work, she has been named a national semifinalist in both the Intel and Siemens-Westinghouse national science research competitions, led her high school academic team to two state championships and been one of two delegates from her state to participate in the U.S. Senate Youth Program. A graduate of North High School in Evansville, Indiana, she is now studying physics at Harvard University.

A Lesson for Both of Us

June pursed her lips and furrowed her brow as I plunged into yet another problem demonstrating least common denominators. Recognizing June's confusion and exasperation, I wracked my brain for a simpler approach, but as I spoke, the blank expression on June's face foretold my impending failure. I waited hopefully as she puzzled over the final step, but she dropped her pencil and sighed, "Negative numbers just don't make sense!"

Clearly, June was frustrated. So was I. All my life, I had ceaselessly soaked up knowledge from books and asked questions about everything around me. I explored new ideas; I pushed myself to achieve and to learn far more than my classes required; and when it came to math, I would gladly spend days pondering a challenging problem. Why couldn't this girl be more like I am? Or at least more like my other pupils? My other math students studied faithfully; my freshman debaters shared insightful new arguments with me daily; even little Hernando, whom I tutored in inner-city Chicago, had been thrilled to have a friend who would study with him.

Part of me wanted to give up on June, but then I realized that some of my own difficult experiences, which had shaped me greatly, could help me to help June. I recalled my painful rejection from the first grade "select choir."

That experience, although it had taught me to accept failures with grace and learn from them, had still hurt terribly, so I resolved never to let anyone label June a failure at math. I also recalled my determination to make the eighth grade volleyball team and the countless hours I spent lifting weights and repeatedly serving the volleyball alone in my backyard before I earned a school uniform. Recognizing the persistence necessary to achieve something difficult, I determined to work my hardest until June mastered her algebra. Finally, I recalled my enthusiastic middle school teacher whose coaching helped and inspired me to win local MATHCOUNTS competitions, qualify for the state team and advance with my teammates to place second nationally. Seeing the value of a committed, motivated, enthusiastic teacher who puts more faith in you than you put in yourself, I promised myself that, despite my frustration, I would not give up on my student.

As I move on to college and beyond, I intend to excel, but more importantly, I want my endeavors to have a positive influence on others. As I work toward this end, I am thankful for my talents and my successes; however, I recognize that some of the greatest gifts I can offer are the perseverance, humility, compassion or strength arising from apparent defeat. Drawing on my natural abilities and life's lessons, I can continue to help others as I helped June, whose blank looks turned to expressions of understanding, whose signs of frustration became promising smiles and who, though I still have much to teach her, finally believes she can succeed.

Career Plans or Field of Study

Danny Fortson, Rotary International Ambassadorial Scholarship Winner

Danny applied for the Rotary scholarship as a way of not only studying journalism but also doing so abroad. He will use the award to gain formal training in journalism and to continue his studies in Spanish. A graduate of U.C. Santa Barbara, Danny's experiences include writing for two San Francisco-based publications, studying abroad in Costa Rica and interning for the Center for Strategic and International Studies, a foreign policy think tank. He thinks he won the award because of his persistence. An unsuccessful applicant the previous year, he used the time in between to increase his qualifications with more journalism experience which is clearly evident in his essay.

International Journalism

Several months ago, I walked into the local bicycle shop, picked out one of the few two-wheelers that fit my lanky frame, strapped a Styrofoam helmet to my head, and set about riding my bike to work every day through the hectic downtown San Francisco traffic. I did not do this out of a strange compulsion to tempt fate but because the day prior I had signed up for the California AIDSRide, a 575-mile, week-long sojourn from San Francisco to Los Angeles to raise money for AIDS treatment and awareness. When I first heard about the event, I had trepidation: "Why not just drive your car? There is no way I'm going to ride my bike more than 500 miles in one week!"

However, I was drawn to the event not only by the desire to challenge myself but to serve a worthy cause. It is these guiding principles, to always push myself and to impact people beyond my own circle, that I look to for direction in all the things I do and something that I feel journalism fulfills. That is why I have chosen to pursue it as a profession, because to be able to write news that is relevant to people's lives is a way to tangibly serve society.

My primary job is as a reporter at *The Daily Deal*, a financial newspaper aimed at investment bankers, corporate lawyers and company executives. Knowing nothing of the complexities of the financial world, I was thrown into the job initially as an editorial assistant, which required me to write authoritatively for a very sophisticated audience. After about three months of intensive learning, I moved up from my post as an editorial assistant to reporter. It was and still is a daunting task, especially with the daily four-hour deadline, but I love the challenge.

My work as a freelance reporter at The Independent Newspaper Group, on the other hand, provides a whole new set of challenges and resplendent rewards. For The Independent I cover stories with a human aspect, issues that are relevant to the people of the local community. Whether I am covering the community service of a local congregation or the phenomenon of the ever-popular scooter, I enjoy the work because I can engage with people in the community and talk about issues important to them.

Working for two drastically different publications, I have learned that so much is determined by larger economic and political factors, but that it all ultimately trickles down to people on the local level. Making that connection with the community is incredibly rewarding, and to be able to extend my reach to a wider audience but retain the local interest is what I am ultimately aiming to do. A year abroad would provide the crucial stepping-stone toward that end.

Of course, the issues affecting local communities are most tangible when you experience them first hand through interactions with its less fortunate, something I have always sought.

In Costa Rica, I found myself at the other end of this teacher-student spectrum. The seven months I spent living and studying at The University of Costa Rica were my first experience as a foreigner in a foreign land. Staying with a local family and attending university classes, I had no choice but to learn Spanish, and fast, at a level that six years of classroom instruction did not afford. In addition, I was in the middle of a crash course in Central American culture and the pertinent issues to the people there, and it was that experience of fully delving into Costa Rican life that imbued me with a passion for the region.

I took that passion to Washington D.C. where I worked as an intern for The Center for Strategic and International Studies, a foreign policy think tank. While there, I worked for The Mexico Project, a program that brought together dignitaries from both sides of the border to foster a unified binational policy. My time in Guatemala also is what fueled my desire to work closely with the Americas Program director to coauthor an election study of that country's presidential race that was disseminated throughout Capitol Hill. Writing that piece for a crowd so far removed from the issues highlighted what I have found to be a recurring dichotomy between the local concerns of one community and the disconnect with a potential audience so many miles away. That is the gap I want to be able to bridge.

It has been three years since I used Spanish in my daily life in Costa Rica, and I desperately want to reach the level of fluency necessary to use in a public forum. In seeking to go abroad once more I intend to do so, as well as get the formal journalistic education to buttress my practical training. Moreover, I could absorb the sense of a foreign society, history and culture that is only attainable through living the daily experience of another country. I would then be equipped to communicate more effectively and to a much wider audience, taking into account the sensibilities of another people and culture and balancing that with the knowledge I have from my own.

Cecilia A. Oleck, Knight Ridder Minority Scholar

Cecilia has competed athletically on the court, field and track. But it's her sense of competition in the newsroom that makes her want to pursue a career in journalism. While a student at West Catholic High School in Grand Rapids, Michigan, she wrote for the newspaper, tackling topics such as the double standards for athletes and gender stereotypes. As a result of her journalism experience, she won over $80,000 in awards including the Knight Ridder Minority Journalism Scholarship and a scholarship from the *Detroit Free Press*, where she has worked as an intern. A student at Saint Mary's College in South Bend, Indiana, she is majoring in communications, preparing for a career in journalism.

The Right Fit

For more people, the future is uncertain; the direction their life will take is not spelled out for them. Each person is responsible for the choices she will make that will determine the course of her life. One of the choices that has an incredible impact on her life is what she will choose for her career.

This can be a difficult decision to make, as it will affect almost every aspect of a person's life to some degree. Most people are also not fortunate enough to receive a startling revelation directing them on the right course for their lives. Instead, the most powerful way that a person is able to determine her direction is not through an earthshaking revelation but through the quiet confidence that this is what she is called to do and to be.

In the same way, I have never received any startling revelations that I should pursue a career in journalism, but as I look back on my life, I am able to see that there were many little steps along the way that have led me to this choice. I have often heard my parents tell the story of how, on my first day of kindergarten, I came home crying because I had not been taught how to read. I have always loved to read and from that has developed a great respect and fascination for the written word.

Joseph Pulitzer stated the purpose of a journalist should be to "Put it before them briefly so they will read it, clearly so they will appreciate it, picturesquely so they will remember it, and above all, accurately so they will be guided by its light." His words serve as a reminder for me of the many different dimensions of writing. Journalism encompasses both creativity and technicality. It is a way of expressing individuality and of communicating with others.

Many of my personal qualities convince me that a career in journalism is my calling. I find that I am a person who responds well to challenges. Perhaps it is because of my competitive nature that challenges motivate me, and I discover that my biggest competitor is usually myself. I think this is why I enjoy trying to combine both the creative and technical aspects of writing. Each time I begin to write, I am presented with a fresh challenge.

Every day that I live, I realize more the impact other people have on me and the impact I have on them. Writing is a very personal way of reaching out to people I may never meet, but who I am still connected to because of our identities as human beings. Journalism allows the opportunity for the sharing of information, thoughts, feelings and ideas between people from all walks of lives. It enables people to see things through another's eyes and gain new perspectives on the world around them.

It is because of the many dimensions of journalism that I desire to pursue a career in this field. I feel that as a journalist, I will be able to use the talents that I already have, as well as learn new ones. I believe it is a chance for me to be an instrument to bring people together.

Chris Kennedy, National Merit Semi-Finalist

From Leawood, Kansas, Chris has always been around animals. He has volunteered at a wildlife rehabilitation center, studied butterflies and moths and worked for his family's canine rescue group. In the ninth grade, Chris and his parents decided that he should be home-schooled so he could better pursue his interests. In addition to studying at home, he has remained active in local science groups and taken courses from a charter high school and college. With this essay on his plans to become an avian veterinarian, he was recognized as a National Merit Semi-Finalist. He gives this advice on applying for scholarships: "Don't put it off. The closer it gets to the deadline, the more terrifying it becomes. So start now."

Avian Veterinarian

I am the only person I know who dreams of becoming an avian veterinarian. That's a bird doctor if your Latin is rusty. I got my first bird—a cockatiel named Sunny for his cheerful disposition—slightly over a year ago. One look into those sweet, intelligent eyes, and I was hooked.

I first gained experience caring for birds of prey, songbirds and waterfowl volunteering with Operation Wildlife, a wildlife rehabilitation and education center that serves the eastern half of Kansas. One particularly memorable day at the center had me tube-feeding a hummingbird. I also participate in the Idalia Society, a group of lepidopterists that studies butterflies, moths and their environments. The magic of nature has always fascinated me, and I am lucky to have found a passion that will let me explore the world of birds and nature in my eventual career.

After seventh grade I chose unorthodox schooling that allowed me to explore my avian interests in more depth while still covering all academic subjects at an advanced level. I have thus pursued a blend of home-school, public school and college coursework. Each year's educational program has been different. In ninth grade I chose a year of home-schooling in literature and world history complemented with work at the college level in geology and biology at Johnson County Community College and volunteering with Operation Wildlife and Farley's Angels, my family's private canine-rescue effort.

At the end of that year I decided I wanted to earn a Kansas Regent's high school diploma but also wanted to continue working at my own pace, exploring topics with greater depth than might be possible in a high school classroom. Those goals came together at Basehor-Linwood Virtual Charter School. I am completing the four-year curriculum in three years, substituting college courses in the sciences. Thanks to the Basehor-Linwood program I have had the latitude to pursue my interest in one facet of my heritage by substituting three years of intensive immersion education in Norwegian for more traditional language programming. At home, I'm currently completing Cornell Ornithology Lab's Bird Biology distance learning course, the University of Missouri-Columbia honors physics course and continuing my volunteer work.

My hard work earned me prizes in physics in the Kansas City Science Fair, in science and social studies in the State of Kansas Scholarship Contest and recognition at the national level by Duke University's Talent Identification (TIP) Program. My unusual curriculum allowed me to compete with students from traditional academic backgrounds while serving my interests as no public school could.

Boy Scouts gave me the chance to enjoy the outdoors while learning about myself and others and gaining valuable leadership skills. I applied those leadership lessons last summer in the American Legion Boys' State of Kansas, a once-in-a-lifetime opportunity to learn about state government. Together these programs taught me about the importance of individual participation and good leadership in groups.

At the most basic level my goals are like those of many others. I want to find the best college environment, study my chosen field of biology or pre-veterinary medicine, go to graduate school and have a fulfilling career. Of course, my particular career goal—to start my own avian veterinary clinic—is unusual, but it serves the same human need. I hope to be a good husband and father, to learn from mistakes, help others and do the right thing while remaining young at heart. With my preparation thus far and a lot more hard work, I will achieve my goals.

Andrea Setters, Dow Scholarship Winner

While she had always known that her future was in the sciences, it took an inspiring teacher for Andrea to discover that her passion was for chemistry. Her teacher at Fairborn High School in Fairborn, Ohio, taught her about the laws of thermodynamics, periodic trends, redox reactions and moles, and in doing so also became a mentor and friend. Andrea says about her teacher, "She brought out the best in me."

Andrea, majoring in chemistry, won scholarships including the Dow Chemistry Scholarship and Furman Founder's Scholarship to attend Furman University in South Carolina. She hopes to eventually earn a Ph.D. and work in pharmaceutical research.

Scientific Inspiration

I often sit in front of blank pieces of notebook paper and half-finished applications wondering why in the world I am still doing all this, wishing it were all over a little sooner. After all, basket weavers make a nice living: they create wonderful pieces with both aesthetic and functional purposes and I bet they didn't have to fill out 20-page questionnaires about what they have done with every waking hour of their lives for the last four years. Then again, I don't have any desire to be a basket weaver. Honestly, I would not have the slightest clue how to begin a basket and I hate splinters. I do, however, have a love of chemistry and it is this love that pushes me to continue with all the forms and essays with a little more enthusiasm than I may have started them with.

When I began to consider future careers, I set two basic criteria: I had to be decent at it, and it had to be something I never seemed to grow tired of. Science became the obvious answer. The not-so-easy question became what I wanted to do with science and what specific discipline. Then, during my sophomore and junior years, two experiences helped narrow down my field: my chemistry classes and being a teaching aide.

When I signed up for honors chemistry, I had absolutely no idea what I was getting myself into. I soon discovered, however, that I had nothing to worry about. The guidance gods smiled on me when they were assigning classes and I was placed in Mrs. Roshto's class. Mrs. Roshto's teaching ability and knowledge of chemistry continue to amaze me to this day. She had the knack to get to know each of her students personally and then be able to offer individual direction. I progressed through the class in a constant state of awe with the new world that was being opened to my eyes each day. I knew chemistry was the field I wanted to devote the rest of my life to.

My junior year I took AP Chemistry, which was also taught by Mrs. Roshto, and during my study hall I aided her Chemistry I class. The positive influence Mrs. Roshto had over so many students was inspiring and I fell in love with the idea that I could introduce students to this world of chemistry that they never could have imagined before. It was during that year that I decided teaching would become one of my career aspirations.

I have solved part of my original dilemma by finding that chemistry is the scientific field I want to work with most. I have yet to discover that perfect career but I believe with classroom experience and guidance I can find it and be able to devote myself to it wholeheartedly.

Essays about Leadership

Swati Deshmukh, Discover Card Tribute Award Scholarship Winner

Swati has helped collect 500 pairs of shoes for hurricane victims in India, raised funds for flood victims in Venezuela and spearheaded a bottled water sale fundraiser to aid flood victims in Mozambique. And these are just some of her efforts abroad.

At home at East Lyme High School in Connecticut, Swati has committed herself to public service, crocheting blankets for premature babies, tutoring students who are refugees from Burma and organizing a book drive for needy libraries.

It is her service and leadership that helped her become one of the nine national winners of the Discover Card Tribute Award. In addition to volunteering, Swati has won numerous awards for her writing, including first place in her state for the National History Day competition. Academically, she has a passion for research, studying organic synthesis of piezoelectric molecules as a participant in NASA's Sharp Program. She would like to eventually attend medical school.

A Fight against Discrimination

One good example of my continuing leadership is my efforts to diminish prejudice and spread feelings of well-being throughout the school. Nearly all of the students who attend my school are white, and I am in a very small minority. For this reason, I feel almost obliged or rather chosen to carry the torch and lead the warriors of unbiased acceptance in an endless war against discrimination.

At the end of my freshman year, I wrote a proposal for a Multi-Cultural Club to recognize and celebrate the minorities at our school. However, the school felt that this subject was covered by other clubs. Disagreeing with the administration, a faculty member at my school invited me to visit Westbrook High School where the Anti-Defamation League was running its program "Names Can Really Hurt Us."

Amazed at what I saw, I labored to bring this program to my school to combat our problems. I convinced my principal to let the Anti-Defamation League come to our school, and I raised the $4,500 that was necessary. With faculty members and other students, I formed the Diversity Team to help run the program. We selected 30 students to form the team, which would be trained by the ADL to help lead the program.

Now, every other week, I run meetings for the Diversity Team in which we prepare for the program. I have set up an e-mail system to contact them, and I have organized a special retreat for us. I also initiated a paper chain project in which every student in the school was given a slip of paper to decorate. The slips of paper will be linked together to form a chain.

My efforts to combat prejudice in the school have turned me into a leader of my peers. In guiding and directing others, I have discovered that I have the ability to lead others and motivate them to achieve great things. I plan to continue my leadership and maintain diversity programs at our school.

Academic Accomplishments

Jonathan Bloom, National Merit Scholarship Winner

When applying for the National Merit Scholarship, Jonathan chose to write about the subject for which he has the most passion—mathematics. While still a student at West Bloomfield High School in Michigan, he took college level math courses and conducted research through an internship with General Motors. He advises other students applying for awards to write about their interests. He says, "They have many students to choose from so you can't be too modest or you won't stand out. Be excited, tell them your passions and write with a goal in mind." Jonathan is studying mathematics at Harvard University and plans to pursue a career in the field. In addition to math, he enjoys tae kwon do, volunteering at a student-run homeless shelter and juggling knives, torches and balls.

Cryptography & Encryption

I would like to pursue an academic life in the field of mathematics. This interest in mathematics developed not only through my coursework but more importantly through my independent research. After successfully completing AP Calculus BC and AP Physics as a sophomore, I felt the need for a greater challenge than that derived from "spoon-fed" instruction. Therefore, the following summer, I attended the Ross Young Scholars Program at Ohio State University. While fully immersed in number theory for eight weeks, I developed a burning hunger for the in-depth study of mathematics. I learned how to think scientifically and perform research independently. The founder of the program honored me with an invitation to return as a junior counselor.

During my junior year, I used a graduate text to guide my research in one of the most active fields of applied number theory, cryptography. My investigation into both public and private key cryptosystems led to an award-winning science project through the development of software, which demonstrated RSA and other encryption algorithms. I completed my directed study in the area of cryptography for 500-level credit at Wayne State University.

Last summer, instead of returning to Ohio State, I completed an internship in the Operations Research Department of the General Motors Truck Group. I conducted a study that identified the most efficient method for accurately approximating the vehicle weight distribution for their product lines. Ten weeks later, I had completed the project, documented the results and given five presentations to increasing levels of management. General Motors is now looking at ways to quickly implement my findings, which will result in the company saving millions of dollars. The vice president has requested that I return next summer.

Currently, in addition to taking 400- and 500-level math courses, I am conducting an independent study at the University of Michigan-Dearborn. I am constructing the first small-scale prototype of "The Weizmann Institute Key Locating Engine" (TWINKLE). As described by Adi Shamir in 1998, this device utilizes optoelectronics to factor large integers presently considered not factorable, effectively threatening the security of 512-bit RSA encryption. The project requires extensive knowledge in mathematics, computer science and electrical engineering. My research has the full support of my faculty advisor, a Ph.D. in mathematics and professor in the CIS department. Professors at three universities have expressed an interest in my progress. Even if I don't reach my goal of a working model for the science fair this spring, I will still have amassed a tremendous amount of knowledge.

As chairman of our school's Science Research Committee and president of the National Honor Society, I have the opportunity to personally encourage classmates to do independent research and to facilitate their entry into the Science and Engineering Fair of Metropolitan Detroit. I hope that I am able to instill into some of my classmates even a fraction of the enthusiasm and motivation that I gained from the Ross Young Scholars Program. With the desire in place, the opportunities are endless.

Note: Jonathan makes one clarification about his essay. He was able to construct only part of the TWINKLE device. However he says, it wasn't "such a disappointment. It's just that my original goal was a little too ambitious."

Svati Singla, Discover Card Tribute Award Scholarship Winner

11-Year-Old Scientist

As an active and innovative student, I am always seeking unique opportunities that will broaden my realm of experience. At a very early age, I became involved in the field of scientific research as a very unique endeavor.

Though I was only 11 years old, I was determined not to let my age hinder my extreme ambition and interest in higher level research. Thus, I independently contacted the head of the Nuclear Cardiology Department at the local university and requested the opportunity to conduct research in his laboratory. Recognizing my genuine interest and scientific aptitude, he immediately introduced me to the lab methods and I began a detailed study, which demanded many hours of my time.

Since I was extremely young, I found the research concepts to be very difficult in the beginning; however, with determination and a positive mental outlook, I was able to comprehend all the research methods. The findings of my research were very significant and were published in the *American Journal of Hypertension*.

After the conclusion of this study, I continued my interest in research by initiating another experimental study in the Department of Biochemistry. This study dealt with drug abuse during pregnancy and fetal alcohol syndrome. The research was presented at local science competitions and was awarded top honors by the U.S. Army and Navy.

Another challenging activity, which I initiated, was to coach a young Odyssey of the Mind team. Odyssey of the Mind is a program that encourages creative thinking, problem solving, and teamwork; I have been involved in this program for over six years and have found it to be a rewarding experience. Thus, when a group of interested first and second graders needed a coach for their team, I readily stepped up and volunteered to accept this massive responsibility. It is very rare for students to coach Odyssey of the Mind teams. Thus, this was a very creative and unique endeavor, which I initiated for the benefit of the young team. Though it was a strenuous time commitment, I obtained a priceless feeling of satisfaction knowing that this had been a positive experience for everyone who was involved.

Both of these unique endeavors have taught me that age should never be a hindrance in the way of learning or sharing knowledge with others.

Seeking Genuineness
Coca-Cola Scholars Foundation

You may think that with the right mix of perseverance and success you can create a winning essay. The truth is that there is no single winning formula for creating a masterpiece. As you'll see in comments from the Coca-Cola Scholars Foundation, the best thing that you can do in your essay is be yourself. —Gen and Kelly

Beyond the essay topic provided, students participating at the Semifinalist level are given no instruction as to how to write their essays for the Coca-Cola Scholars Foundation's four-year Scholars Program.

"We don't provide instruction because we see the essay as an opportunity for each student to sincerely express themselves," says Trisha Bazemore, program assistant.

The 27 members of the Program Review Committee, comprised of college admission officers and high school guidance counselors, are chosen for their expertise in evaluating students' writing.

So what is the committee seeking as it reviews the 2,000 Semifinalist applications? In a word, genuineness.

"You can tell when you read an essay if it's 'real,' expressing an individual's heartfelt experience, or if it's an essay derived more from an awareness of presentation," says Bazemore. She says that it's important that students not try to write what they think the review committee wants to read.

"Be yourself," she says.

Emily Heikamp, Angier B. Duke Memorial Scholarship Winner

When exploring colleges in high school, it took Emily and her mother 14 hours to drive from Metairie, Louisiana, to the North Carolina campus of Duke University. But it was time well spent. After her visit, Emily fell in love with the college. She later wrote this essay to gain admission to and earn a full-tuition scholarship from Duke. In all, the self-described "science nerd" earned over $250,000 in scholarships including full-tuition awards from Texas A&M and Tulane University, which she declined to attend her dream school. A graduate of Archbishop Chapelle High School, she is majoring in biology and mathematics and plans to earn an M.D.Ph.D. in immunology or oncology.

Science Nerd

AGTCCGGAATT is the genetic code for Tumor Necrosis Factor (TNF), a human cytokine that may have deleterious, even fatal effects if produced in excess or inadequate quantities. For the past two years, I have performed research to study the effects of alcohol and glucocorticoids on the TNF response in murine macrophage cells. One may ask why I am interested in such an obscure topic. Well, I am a science nerd.

Scientific research fascinates me, as experiments raise many questions and always provide new challenges. Research also supplies knowledge of the most intimate interactions of the human body, giving a glimpse of processes that are invisible to the naked eye. My research provides me with this knowledge and the ability to share it with others, and it has given my life direction and purpose.

I discovered my passion for research when I was 15 years old. The summer after my sophomore year, I decided to trade in cherished lazy afternoons with tennis buddies, waking up at 1 p.m. and two months of dormancy for my tired brain. I became an employee of the physiology department at Louisiana State University Medical Center. My buddies became lab technicians, I woke up at 7 a.m. instead of sleeping in and my tired brain was forced into overdrive as I learned about Tumor Necrosis Factor and Lipopolysaccharides. And I loved my job.

I worked for Dr. Gregory Bagby, a professor and researcher of the Alcohol Research Center at LSUMC. His lab studies the effects of Simian Immuno-deficiency Virus and Ethanol on Rhesus Macaques. In other words, how SIV-infected drunken monkeys can get really sick. Nonetheless, his research fascinated me, and I had so many questions. Perhaps what fascinated me even more was Dr. Bagby spent time explaining his world of Lipopolysac-charides (LPS) and Tumor Necrosis Factor (TNF) to me, a lowly high school sophomore! I began to perform experiments and assays for his lab, while also doing secretarial work for his research grants. Eventually, I began my own research on alcohol and stress hormones. My research taught me so much and gave my life new direction. I finally knew what career I would pursue. But more importantly, I learned what kind of researcher I want to be. Dr. Bagby had shown me that being a great scientist is more than No-bels, prestige, and grant money. It is about sharing what you have learned with others, even lowly high school sophomores!

Being able to work with others who share my passion and enthusiasm has helped me to shape my dream. I plan to earn an M.D.Ph.D., specializing in immunology. As a physician scientist, I will see patients while also perform-ing research to find new medications or a cure for their illnesses. I feel blessed to be a healthy young woman, and so I want to serve those who are not as fortunate by doing what I love most—research.

Nancy Pan, National Merit Scholar

Nancy is from Covina, California, and was attending South Hills High School when she wrote this essay for the National Merit Scholarship. She has won more than $10,000 in academic scholarships and is currently attending Stanford University. Her advice to students writing personal scholarship essays is to "dig deep within yourself to find something that uniquely represents you. From there show how your actions or achievements illustrate that particular aspect of you. The key is to have both the internal passion and the evidence that supports it."

Superpan

My name is Nancy Pan. Growing up, my parents would always tease me, "You're not Superpan, you know."

But in my mind I was. Not only did I boast a red cape tied across my shoulders, I was also always pushing my limits. At age four, I would secretly practice on the courts for hours with ambitions of beating my six-foot tall dad in basketball. In third grade, I dedicated my entire summer at the library to writing my first 62-page novel, complete with hand illustrations. By the time I entered middle school, I had managed to skip a total of four years in mathematics while remaining #1 in a class with high school juniors.

I am obviously not a superhero, but my life has been characterized by the dual roles which typify one—doing what others expect of me and doing what I expect of myself. It is with my choice to establish a profound difference between the two that I have optimized my high school experience.

These last three years, my academic life has been fueled by my passions for writing and mathematics. In writing, I am fascinated by its polar nature. At school, I've enrolled in Advanced Placement writing courses to understand the objective aspect of writing, dissecting written works based on both the content and presentation of the author's message. I achieved a perfect score on my SAT Verbal and AP Literature exams, but I did not stop at being a good student. Rather, as an individual, I wanted to express myself in a way that was uniquely my own and yet still capable of moving others. I saw the development of my analytical abilities as a means of advancing my true passion, creative writing. Although such writing is more liberated and subjective, it too is built on a similar ability to dissect, analyze and understand plot and theme construction. I exploited what I learned in class, and in my own time, wrote volumes of poetry and short stories. In doing so, I won several city-wide writing contests, a poetry competition with Barnes & Nobles, a local publication and the luxury of putting my soul to words.

Perhaps in a way completely antonymous to my attraction for creative writing, I am fascinated by the objective purity of mathematics. However to me, math is not solely an abstract science but also a way to practically understand the world with numbers. Prior to high school, I extended my knowledge of mathematics outside of class, so that by the time I was a freshman, I had completed the AP Calculus curriculum. My school did not offer an official AP Calculus BC class, so I independently prepared for the exam and received a 5. Outside of class, I am enrolled in community college math courses, active in the Science Bowl with a focus on Mathematics and am additionally, the school representative for the Mathematics Olympiad. Although there are limitations in the math coursework provided by my school, my knowledge and passion for the subject has continued to thrive through my search for and involvement in outside opportunities.

Writing and mathematics are only two examples of areas in which I have recognized my potential to achieve and acted accordingly. However, I am an individual with many working passions. You will find in my application that I am additionally the Captain and All-League Finalist of my Varsity Tennis Team, a Valedictorian candidate, a winner of various scholarships, an active executive/officer in several extracurricular clubs, an avid volunteer, an employed instructor at a learning center and many other positions, each listed neatly but constrainedly upon the allotted line. I am all of these things, but they themselves are simply manifestations of my desire to reach my peak as an individual.

Over the years, my parents adapted their mocking tone and started calling me Superpan with affection. As for me, it's been years since I've put on that red cape again, but my mentality has not waived. I will continue to push my limits only to someday realize that there are none.

Essays about Athletics

Sara Bei, CIF Scholar-Athlete of the Year

From Montgomery High School in Santa Rosa, California, Sara was still excited about her team's underdog victory at the state cross country meet when she wrote this essay. One of the most profound lessons that she learned was how to motivate her team, a topic she uses as the centerpiece of this essay. Along with a half-tuition scholarship to Stanford, Sara also won over $6,000 in scholarships. She encourages all students to be relentless about applying for scholarships since in her words, "sometimes the ones you end up winning are the one you almost didn't apply to."

Inspiring Greatness

As a three-time state cross country champion entering my senior year, I hadn't expected this season to be much different than the others. I planned on working hard to achieve my goal of winning state, and I looked forward to having fun with my teammates in the process. In previous years, our girls' team hadn't been very motivated, leaving me to take it upon myself to make it to state as an individual. Little did I know that a completely different challenge lay ahead of me for my senior year.

At the beginning of the year, I was pleasantly surprised to find two newcomers fresh out of junior high, who had decided to come out for the team to give us the fourth and fifth runners that we so desperately needed. Immediately I began to ponder what our team's potential was, and as always, I shot high. I organized a team sleep-over and, while beading necklaces and watching movies, tried to instill in them the goal of winning the state championship. Most of them were doubtful, even shocked, that I thought a team who failed to even make it to the state meet the previous year could have a shot at winning it. However, I was prepared to help them to not only realize their potential and believe in themselves, but to work together as a group and strengthen one another in the process.

Throughout the road to the state meet, I was busy trying to find ways to motivate the girls to train harder. I gave them little weekly gifts and notes, made breakfast as incentive for morning runs before school, organized team bonding activities outside of practice and even made a "State Champion Challenge Chart." I tried everything possible to get them to do the necessary preparation to be the best, as well as have fun and come together as a team. In the process, I found myself devoting so much time to the team that I was hardly channeling any energy into my own training. Although this concerned my coach, I reassured her that by working with the team, we were helping each other and improving together.

Finally, the day arrived in a flutter of nerves, anxiety and excitement. After giving them a pep talk, we toed the line together and I thought back on all the months we spent training, planning and dreaming for this moment. True, I was out to become the first person to win four state titles, but as I chanted our cheer with each of the girls, I realized that my real drive to win was coming from our team's need for every point we could get. That day, we upset the first- and second-ranked teams, with each girl running the race of her lifetime to become the Division II State Champions! Seeing the smiles and tears of pure joy on the faces of my teammates, I realized that beyond the medals and championships, there lies a treasure of value that far surpasses any other individual award in inspiring greatness in others.

Artistic Talents

Andrew Koehler, Fulbright Grant Winner

Andrew has been a serious student of music since he was 5 years old, when he first began to play the violin. Originally from Oreland, Pennsylvania, he has performed as a violinist with the Philadelphia Youth Orchestra, the Yale Symphony Orchestra and numerous festival orchestras. While at Yale, from which he graduated with honors as a double German Studies and Music major, he began to conduct seriously and is now pursuing a career in conducting. After spending a summer as a conducting student at the Aspen Music Festival and School, he is continuing his studies at the University for Music and Art in Vienna on a Fulbright Grant.

Turningpoint

My parents both spent the first part of their childhood overseas. As Ukrainian immigrants in America, they faced both the immediate difficulty of learning a new language and the eventual difficulty of acting as translators for their families, who never were able to learn English adequately. Though I, too, was raised speaking Ukrainian, my parents ultimately wanted to give me a means of communication that would transcend all others, a language of international recognition; this, they decided, was to be music.

The choice they gave me, for whatever reason, consisted of only two instruments: violin and piano. Such was the decision I was to make at the age of 5, when I might otherwise have been happier to continue playing uninterruptedly with my action figures. I arbitrarily chose violin, blissfully unaware of the impending consequences. I cannot pretend that something in my soul stirred the first time I held the instrument. I played dutifully enough, though I, like any other child, did not really enjoy practicing. I went through a long series of mediocre teachers who failed to generate any real excitement in me. They gave me enough encouragement, however, to realize that I had at least some talent, and with this ray of hope, my parents continued to push me.

Much later, during the first rehearsal of a youth orchestra I had recently joined, something astonishing occurred. Sitting in the back of the section, I was intimidated in part by the music on the stand in front of me but mostly by the conductor on the podium, an extraordinarily temperamental man who could be blisteringly honest in passing judgment on one's abilities as a musician. We began the rehearsal by sight-reading the first piece in our program. We muddled through admirably enough, but he was clearly unsatisfied. He leapt from his stool and spat, "You play like you're older than I am," with each strong syllable of his phrase strengthened by ferocious baton swats on his stand. He paused and composed himself. "Do you know what this music is about?" No one dared breathe a word. He then spoke of love and death and of the profound tragedy that links the two with an eloquence unbefitting his audience. He stopped suddenly and disgustedly offered, "but you don't understand; you're too young," and then looked up at us questioningly, as if to ask whether or not he was right. He might well have been, but we desperately wanted to understand for that man. And so we played again, and this time, I began to hear music in an utterly different way, as did many, I suspect. His passion for this art was simply infectious. Where I had never previously known music to be more than just pleasant, I began to understand what defined greatness, both in interpretation and in composition. Poor performances could make me cringe, but the most sublime moments in great performances made my hair stand on end. I began to approach music with a penetrating enthusiasm which, save for the charisma of a great teacher, might never have been.

Years later, and as my focus shifts from violin to conducting, this enthusiasm continues only to strengthen. Knowing the difficulties of a life in music, I have tried seriously to pursue other interests, but no matter how engaging I find them, none generate the same passion in me that music does. I am resigned to my fate; I wish to be a musician. It is a perilous fate that neither my parents nor certainly I could have imagined when this endeavor began, but it is a fate nevertheless tinged with joy, for I may count myself among the few who have found something they sincerely love.

CHAPTER SIX

12 ESSAYS THAT BOMBED

In this chapter:

- **12 disastrous essays**

- **"Where's the Point"**

- **"Attempted Tearjerker"**

- **"Miss America"**

- **"Behold! My Statistics"**

- **"My Life as Seen on TV"**

Learning from Failure

History has shown that some of our greatest successes have been inspired by failure. Akio Morita's automatic rice cooker was a huge failure and burned the rice it was supposed to boil. In desperation, Morita and a partner turned to building cheap tape recorders. From this single product came Sony Corp. Across the ocean a high school coach cut a young varsity football player. That athlete's name was none other than Michael Jordan. The founder of the automobile industry, Henry Ford twice filed for bankruptcy before he finally stumbled onto the product that would launch his company, the Model T.

In keeping with history's tradition we bring you 12 essays that failed. These essays, however, provide an extremely important lesson: they help you learn what not to do. As you read each essay along with our comments you will understand why they fell short of the mark. While you are writing essays, keep the lessons from this chapter in mind. These essay writers lost the various competitions in which they entered, but at least in doing so they are helping you to avoid the same fate.

Where's the Point?

Reading an essay without a point is like getting on an airplane without knowing where it's going. Yet many students turn in essays without any clear message. Consider the following essay and see if you can locate the message the author is trying to convey:

Where Has Time Gone?

As I sit at the lunch table, it suddenly hits me. Where has all the time gone? I am a senior in high school who is about to graduate in a matter of months and I have just realized that I might never see my friends after we receive our diplomas.

Surely we'll see each other at reunions, but what will become of the great moments that we have shared?

I will never forget when one of my friends and I were given the responsibility of putting together a class beach party. My friend wasn't a very creative or outgoing person, however, he was nearly twice as strong as me. So we came up with a plan. I would do all of the promotion for the party as well as decide the theme and menu. He would be responsible for making sure all of the food, sound equipment and decorations were transported to the beach. It was the perfect plan. Most of our classmates told us afterward that it was the best activity that they'd ever been to.

I sometimes wish I could stay in my school forever. I have learned so much in the last four years. Before I came to high school I didn't even know what I was capable of intellectually. My teachers have been some of the most inspirational people in my life.

I know that college will bring with it many new memories and experiences and I am looking forward to it. However, I will never forget the friends who stayed by my side and the teachers who cared throughout the good times and the bad.

Why This Essay Bombed

In this essay, the author simply has no meaning in his writing. The essay covers a range of feelings and experiences. By the end of the essay we wonder what we just read. Is the point that the author will miss his friends? Is it that he is able to solve the problem of working with a friend who is not creative or outgoing? Or is it that his teachers have been the most influential people in his life? There is no connection between the disjointed ideas. We are left confused and unimpressed.

How to Avoid This Mistake

As you are writing, think about what you are trying to convey. Ask the question, "What's the significance of this essay?" If you can't answer this question in a single sentence, then it probably means you need to make your message stronger and more clearly defined.

Since there is often limited space for the essay, it is better to stick to a single topic. Select one and develop it throughout the essay. Don't confuse the scholarship committee by writing about a number of things that have little or no connection to each other.

The Attempted Tearjerker

There were few dry eyes at the end of the movie "Titanic," and the director wanted it that way. Movies about tragedy are intended to evoke emotion from viewers. Some students do the same thing with their scholarship essay, attempting to win the reader over with dejected accounts of loss, desperation and hopelessness.

Unfortunately, these essays do not appeal to scholarship judges. They do not want to read about how difficult your past has been except within the context of how you've faced the challenges or your plans for improving the situation. They want to be inspired by what you have done and see that you are working to make your life better.

My So-Called Life

Someone once said, "Life is like a bowl of cherries--sometimes it's the pits." There could be no more accurate saying to describe my life thus far.

Even before I was born there was trouble. When my mother was pregnant she got into a car accident and nearly lost her baby--me! While I don't recall this event it was clearly an omen of things to come.

Throughout my childhood my parents were never rich. I remember one Christmas how jealous I was when I went back to school and my friends had the newest clothes and toys. Sure, I got gifts but not the kind of expensive presents that my friends had received.

When I was 15 years old I returned home one day and noticed that something was different. Half of the stuff that we owned in our apartment was gone. We had been robbed. The burglar had taken most of the good stuff that we owned. That year my brothers and I had to share a single 21-inch television.

As if things could not get any worse, the next year I learned that I had diabetes. While not life threatening it was enough to send me into a depression that took months to get out from.

Now that I am about to graduate I feel lucky to even be here given the hardships of my past 17 years. Going to college has been a life-long dream. This scholarship would help me pay for college and build a better life.

Why This Essay Bombed

While it is hard to not feel sympathy for an applicant who has suffered misfortunes and hardships, there are almost no scholarships that give money based on how much you have suffered. Rather scholarship judges want to see how you have excelled despite the obstacles in your life. The focus should be on what you have accomplished or what you plan to accomplish in spite of setbacks.

How to Avoid This Mistake

If the past has been rough, you can certainly write about it. But don't expect the hardships themselves to make your essay a winner. Make sure to include what you have achieved or what you have learned from these challenges. Write about how the hardships will influence your choices or affect the future. While scholarship judges know that many students have had to endure difficulties, what they want to see is someone who has survived and thrived.

Miss America Essay

We've all seen the Miss America Pageants. And we've all heard (and made fun of) the speeches contestants make. "I want to cure the world of hunger," "I want to save and give back to mother nature" and "I want to make sure that every person on the planet has a place they can happily call home." These ideals are just too lofty to take seriously. It is amazing how many scholarship applicants write about these very ideals that, despite their good intentions, are just too idealistic to be considered seriously.

My Dedication to the World

Through five years of community service, I've learned many things. I've seen the empty hearts in the children without parents and the broken hearts of seniors who get no visitors. Because of these experiences, I've learned that only through service I can be a fulfilled person.

Therefore, I have decided to work to end the suffering of all people who face the perils of being without food, clothing or shelter. This is now my life goal.

After college I plan to start a shelter for orphans. This orphanage will take care of children who have been abandoned and will attempt to create as normal a family life as possible. Once my first orphanage is established I will branch out to other areas and countries. My dream is to build a global network that would once and for all end the suffering of children.

Once I have accomplished this I plan on running for public office so that I can affect change on an even broader scale. As senator or president I will make laws and convince other countries to do what they can to protect each and every human. For it is only by committing ourselves to ending human suffering that progress can be made.

As humans we are here to make the world a better place, and if each person does his or her part, like I plan to do, the world *would* be a much better place.

Why This Essay Bombed

The applicant's heart is in the right place but the ideas are just too farfetched to be taken seriously. This just sounds too much like a Miss America answer and does not show that the applicant has any basis in reality.

How to Avoid This Mistake

This type of essay should be avoided altogether. There's no doubt that if each of us were given the chance, we would end worldwide hunger or save Mother Nature, but let's face it, this isn't realistic. Focusing on a few issues and describing what you have done can make a great essay. Keep a positive attitude and enthusiasm but ground your ideas in reality, and focus on what you have done instead of what you would do in a limitless world.

The Life-Changing Voyage

Whether backpacking across Europe or climbing Mt. McKinley, there are those students who have traveled the world. A part of their experience is the wealth of memories they brought back home. Thus, travel is a common topic when it comes to essays. However, essays about travel too often make sweeping generalizations, depict the superficial aspects of the trip or cover the events of two weeks in two pages. Here is an example of a travel essay gone awry:

My Trip to Europe

Two years ago I had the privilege of traveling to six European countries. There I met many interesting people and saw many interesting sights. In England I got to stand next to the guard who cannot be disturbed from his upright, staring position. In France I got to look out to the horizon from the famous Eiffel Tower. In Belgium I ate frites, which are essentially Belgian french fries. In Germany I saw where the Berlin Wall stood not too many years ago. In Italy I saw the Colosseum, where the Gladiators fought. And finally, in Switzerland I saw the Alps and ate fondue.

Besides having a great time seeing new places and meeting new faces, I also learned a great deal about the cultures of different European countries. I learned that people from different countries are, well, different. They have different mindsets about certain aspects of life and different ways of thinking. However, I also learned that people are, in a way, all the same. All the different ideas and concepts centered on the same areas of thinking and are therefore merely different interpretations of the same thing.

My visit to Europe has definitely changed my view of the world. I hope that someday everyone will have a chance to visit Europe or another foreign land and learn how diverse and similar our world really is.

Why This Essay Bombed

This essay is too much of a diary of sights seen, activities done and food eaten. Virtually *any* student who visited Europe could have written this—and many will. The essay also makes a general observation of travelers—that while people from different countries have differences we are all essentially the same. The result is that this essay hardly stands out from any other essay about travel.

How to Avoid This Mistake

Whether your travels have taken you to the Museé du Louvre in Paris or your grandmother's house in Tulsa, you probably have numerous experiences that could become good essays. However, when you're considering the possibilities, try to separate those events that could happen to many travelers from those that were truly unique to your visit. Focus on a specific event and elaborate on what it has taught you or how it has affected your life. Instead of writing about all seven days of travel, narrow it to one day or even one hour. Also avoid sweeping generalizations about the people of a country or humanity at large.

Convoluted Vocabulary

How many times have you read a passage in a standardized test or in an advanced work of literature and found that each word made you more confused than the last? If used properly, word choice can convey sophistication and demonstrate a writer's command of the language. However, when used incorrectly or only to impress, the results are convoluted, conceited or just plain incorrect. Here is an example of an essay that was intended to awe. See if you are impressed enough with this writer to hand over *your* money.

Educationality

That education is my utmost priorative focus is verified in my multitude of academic, extracurricular and intercurricular activities. I insinuate myself in learning and acquiring a plethora of knowledge. I am a person that doesn't approbate no for an answer when it comes to enhancing the prominence of my mind.

This pontifical accolade is an integral part of my scholarization, and without it, my temperament would fall short of instructured. My transcendent achievements speak for themselves and deserve accolades.

Why This Essay Bombed

It appears as if this essay had a head-on collision with a thesaurus. Using SAT words is fine as long as you use them correctly. Scholarship judges are not interested in how complicated a sentence you can construct, but rather how meaningful you can make it. Plus, some of the words this applicant uses were made up!

How to Avoid This Mistake

Don't venture into areas of the English language where you are a stranger. It is okay to use multisyllabic words when you see fit, but to use big words just for the sake of using them is a mistake.

Behold! My Statistics

Have you ever read the back of a baseball card? It is filled with statistics reflecting the player's performance during the season. It may show that a player is one of the fastest men on the field or that he performs well in the playoffs, but the statistics say nothing about a player as a person. Keep this in mind when writing scholarship application essays. If you just list statistics such as GPA, classes and activities, the judges will never get meaningful insight into who you really are.

My Name Is Brooke

Hello, my name is Brooke. I will be a senior at Central High School in Topeka, Kansas.

I was born on October 29. I have interests in writing and mathematics. My schedule junior year was as follows: AP English Language, Honors Physics, AP Calculus AB, AP United States History, Honors III Spanish and P.E. My extracurricular activities are varsity cheer and Key Club.

Here are my standardized test scores: 1270 SAT, 620 SAT Literature Subject Test, 610 SAT US History Subject Test, 680 SAT Math Level 2 Subject Test, 4 on AP English, 3 on AP US History and 3 on AP Calculus.

I have worked hard throughout my four years in high school to maintain a 3.7 GPA. I plan to graduate with honors next year. From there I will go to college.

I plan to major in either communications or business in college. The reason I will major in either communications or business is because I love to work with people and I am seriously interested in getting into the entertainment industry.

My favorite subjects in school this past year were AP English and AP Calculus. My hobbies include sewing, playing piano, singing and writing short stories. I currently have a job at a local restaurant.

Why This Essay Bombed

This essay gives a great deal of information about the writer but it says almost nothing about her motivation, dreams or beliefs. Qualities that show your character are the ones in which scholarship judges are most interested. They want a sense of who you are. This isn't conveyed through a list of statistics. Also, the application often asks for most of this information. So why repeat a list of activities, classes and GPA when the scholarship judges already have your application and transcript?

How to Avoid This Mistake

It's easy to write an essay in which you rattle off your status in life and a list of accomplishments. What's more difficult is putting your place in life and achievements into perspective and making sense of them. Focus on a few of the more important achievements and expand on those. Since the application form has a place to list activities, grades and test scores, don't repeat that information in the essay. Use the essay to go beyond your statistics and provide context for their significance.

The Most Influential Person in the World

A common essay topic is the person who has had the most influence on your life. You can imagine the countless essays that students write about parents, grandparents, siblings, friends and idols. The challenge is to write about this influential person in a way that is different from what other students write and that reveals something about you as well. This essay falls short on both counts.

I Love My Family

There is no one person who has had the most influence in my life; instead, it is a group. That group consists of the most important people in my life: my family. My family is made up of four people: my mom, my dad, my younger sister and me. My parents are my role models; they provide the home in which I live, the food that I eat and the money to buy essential items. They have set for me a good example of what kind of life I should lead. They have always been there for me, through the good times and the bad, to support, love and cherish me.

My mom, in particular, has always been very supportive of me. She has been the one to tell me bedtime stories when I go to sleep. She has been my unacknowledged chauffeur, taking me places such as the occasional baseball game or regular piano lesson even if she had more important things to do.

My father, on the other hand, has always been the advice giver. To me, he is all knowing, for he always has a good answer to the questions I have. My father, who is an engineer, helps me with my math and science homework; I wouldn't be as successful at math if it weren't for him. I love both my parents because they have both contributed to my life so much.

My sister has also played an important role in my life. She has always helped me whenever I was in need; when I couldn't solve a problem, when I couldn't think of a good design for my visual aid or just when I needed someone to talk to. I love my sister, and even though I'd be embarrassed to tell it to her face, she's my best friend. And even though we might fight every so often about issues we shouldn't even care about, our friendship is a strong one; those fights are just testaments to how real it really is.

Why This Essay Bombed

The problem with this essay is that it is too ordinary. Many applicants will write about what their parents do for them and how they hope to pattern their lives after them. This essay just does not stand out.

How to Avoid This Mistake

It may be difficult to choose just one person who stands above the rest. And the person you select may be mom or dad. These essays will work if, and *only* if, a unique angle is taken. A generic description about your father, such as, "My father is always there for me, through the good times and the bad," will go nowhere. It's important to be as specific as possible in describing exactly what it is that you admire about your father. Fortunately, there are unique things about all of our siblings, parents, friends and idols that make them special. Focus on those aspects.

Creativity Overload

We've all heard the various analogies for life—"life is like a box of chocolates," "life is a sport" and so on. Wouldn't it be clever if, somehow, you could create your *own* analogy of life? Surely it would show how deep of a thinker you are and how well you can write, right? Being clever is usually good. But sometimes it can go too far, wearing out a novel idea.

The Highway of Life

Life is like a highway with cars going in all directions. People are constantly coming and going from all sorts of places. Sometimes, when too many people want to go to the same place, traffic jams form, just as when too many people apply for a single position at a company.

Be True
Elisa Juárez & Emanuel Pleitez

Being truthful in the essay is not just the right thing to do but it also makes for a much better essay. Many essay disasters are created when students decide to write about something they don't know much or care about.—Gen & Kelly

Elisa Tatiana Juárez
Brown University student and scholarship winner
"Be honest. I have a lot of friends who said you could lie. You could but in the end people will really know who you are."

Emanuel Pleitez
Stanford University student and scholarship winner
"Be true. Don't try to fake anyone out. It's not going to work. You don't have to be the greatest writer. I write what I really feel. If you really believe in what you're writing, then you should be well off."

The Highway Patrol is akin to my parents because whenever I feel like breaking the rules, as any driver would, the presence of my parents always prevents me from doing so.

Throughout my young life I have been on a highway full of cars passing interesting exits. As I pass each exit--the doctor exit, the lawyer exit, the CEO exit--I realize that my highway of life is full of so many possibilities.

However, none of these intriguing possibilities can be reached without the integral element of the automobile: gas. In my mind, my education is the gas that will run my car that will take me to these places.

Why This Essay Bombed

The student might think that this concept of comparing life to a highway is quite inspired. In fact, she might have even talked about it with her friends and they might have been impressed. However, somewhere along the line she must have missed adult contact. This essay really just makes the applicant appear silly. She starts with an original idea but takes it too far in an overly simplified way. Being creative is good. But don't go overboard and end up with a laughable essay.

How to Avoid This Mistake

Have several other people read your essay. If you feel that maybe it is too creative or may border on being trite, ask what they think. Sometimes we just get too caught up in our own writing to make good judgments.

The Future Me

Scholarship organizations will often ask applicants where they see themselves in 10 years (or some other time in the not so distant future). Now we know what you're thinking–steady job, happily married, living in a nice house, two adorable children and dog named Spike. Stop right there, because this is your worst enemy. This idea is exactly what the 10,000 other applicants are planning to write about.

But wait a minute, this idea is *also* your best friend. You now have the perfect idea of what *not* to write about, and this information can prove quite useful when it comes to writing an original essay. Here is an example of an essay where the writer falls for this trap:

Ten Years from Now

Ten years from now, I see myself as a college graduate from a local private university. I will also have a steady job at a company for which I love to work. Hopefully I will be married, and, if I am, I'll probably have one or two kids. I plan to spend my free time with my family and maybe indulge in a few sporting events.

My job will probably be as an accountant, and I will give it my best. I'll like my job, because I've always liked to work with numbers. The only drawback will be that an accountant's salary will not be as much as I would desire to make. So I plan to achieve a state of wealth by investing in the stock market. By doing so, I will enable myself to retire at an early age.

In retirement I will continue to invest intelligently in the stock market so I can pay for my children's educations. I will travel the world with my family during the summers and donate to various charitable organizations.

My future will be a bright one provided that I get my own education. Ten years from now, the brightness will just be beginning to unveil, and I will be stepping into the happiest phase of my life.

Why This Essay Bombed

While this may be how the applicant truly feels it makes for one boring essay. It reflects the goals that almost every person has of being successful and happy, making the essay ordinary and unoriginal.

How to Avoid This Mistake

When asked where you see yourself in 10 years, focus on a single desire. You might write about an unfulfilled dream or a specific contribution that you hope to make. To make the essay more interesting, don't approach your future in the same way that nearly every other student will view his or her life. Make the essay interesting by including your motivations, challenges, inspirations, rationale and expectations for the future.

My Life as Seen on TV

The average American spends dozens of hours watching television each week. It's not surprising then that entertainment from television, film and music finds its way into scholarship essays. While entertainment is an influence, it is a mistake to draw parallels to something with which there really is little or no connection. Whatever topic you choose to write about should have a relationship to your life.

Liza

A movie I recently saw struck a heartfelt tone in my mind. I realized that the main character, Liza, was forced to struggle through circumstances similar to mine.

After losing her father in World War II, Liza's mother raised her as a single parent. Through the hardships, Liza's mother grew physically and mentally stronger because she knew she had to make sure that her daughter would be all right. Liza, however, did not appreciate her mother's efforts. Liza was an aspiring actress. Her favorite acting part during her senior year was playing Dorothy in *The Wizard of Oz*, the final play of her high school career.

On the night of the final performance, Liza's mother had a commitment that she could not afford to miss. Liza begged her mother to come in time to hear the last song--a reasonable request--and her mother lovingly promised that she would be there. Liza gave the greatest performance of her life that night and waited patiently for her mother to arrive, until the final song was about to be cued. At that point, Liza began to lose hope, and by the time the song was over she completely hated her mother. Liza waited around after the play until a police officer suddenly pulled up to the school to tell her that her mother had died at the hands of a drunk driver while on her way to the play. Devastated, Liza finally realized how much her mother really loved her.

The movie was especially touching because Liza lived her entire childhood trying to get away from her mother, but lived the remainder of her life appreciating how much her mother actually meant to her. My life story is similar to Liza's because I too am aspiring to be someone, except I aspire to be a psychologist. Also, I have been fortunate enough not to lose either of my parents, although my father has a strenuous work schedule, and I only see him in the mornings.

I have been inspired by this movie to appreciate the love, support and encouragement that my parents have provided for me in the past and which they continue to provide.

Why This Essay Bombed

Touching story, the movie that is. Not only is the writer's life nothing like that of Liza's, the inspiration the writer has received tells us nothing about the writer herself. This essay would work a lot better for someone who *has* suffered such tragedies and hardships.

How to Avoid This Mistake

While choosing a topic, it is fine to select one that shares a touching story, but this story should relate to your life. A good story is entertaining, but a better one gives insight into who you are.

Excuses, Excuses, Excuses

Nobody is perfect. We all make mistakes. Maybe you skipped a few too many 8 a.m. classes in freshman year. Perhaps you didn't put all of your effort into a science project. All of this is normal. However, what is not normal or useful is using the essay to explain past mistakes. The essay should be used to highlight your strengths, not call the judges' attention to or make excuses for your shortcomings.

It's Not My Fault

I received horrible grades all throughout high school, but hardly any of them were due to my own actions. Let me explain: you'll notice that during freshman year I earned a 2.5 GPA. The reason for this is that I had just gone through a difficult move to a new city, the first time our family had relocated. It was hard for me to adjust to the new environment of living in a big city and I made few friends. Because of this, I had a very difficult time in all my classes, which, by the way, were chosen all by my overprotective mother.

Then, during sophomore year, I finally started to make some pretty good friends, but one day in the middle of October, my dog died. That devastated me. I took the SAT I that month and my results definitely reflect this loss. Throughout the year I couldn't recover from such a loss, because I had my dog since I was 5 years old.

Then came junior year. Emotionally, this was my worst year. I went through a terrible breakup with my girlfriend of five months in the middle of winter break. Since then, school has been in the way of my recovery, and I have performed poorly as a result. I tried taking the SAT I again, and my emotional weakness once again reflects my scores. APs and SAT Subject Tests were no different. I joined the basketball team in the beginning of the year, but I was almost immediately cut.

Senior year I tried to make a comeback, but my GPA remained the same. This discouraged me because none of my friends believed I was intelligent.

I tried to join clubs in the hopes that community involvement would cure my woes, but in fact the impersonality of clubs altogether discouraged me further so I haven't stayed in any.

Meanwhile, my family is running out of money. My dad has been laid off from his job for about six months now. I feel like the world is against me now, and I could really use this scholarship to help my college career, if I have one.

Why This Essay Bombed

What this essay does is call attention to the writer's deficiencies instead of his strengths. We all have things about ourselves that we are not proud of so why put faults on display when the object of the scholarship essay is to impress the judges? Compounding this effect is that the student tries to avoid taking responsibility for his shortcomings by blaming everything and everyone else. If you are going to admit to a mistake then at least take responsibility for your actions.

How to Avoid This Mistake

Showcase your strengths in the essay. If you do need to reveal a weakness or shortcoming, explain how you have grown from the experience. We all make mistakes but what is important is that we learn from each of them. Whatever you do, don't avoid responsibility for your actions.

Complex Problem, Simple Solution

Some scholarship essays are about an issue of national or international importance. Scholarship committees often choose topics that ask difficult questions regarding complex issues so that they can discover what is important to you. The judges want to weigh your thoughts and to check your understanding of complicated interests and viewpoints. It would seem fairly obvious that the biggest mistake in writing this type of essay is to know nothing about the problem or to present a wholly unrealistic solution. Observe.

Nuclear Nightmare

Imagine a nuclear nightmare. Bombs exploding. Millions of people vaporized. Entire cities destroyed. This is the reality we face even after the Cold War has been won.

The major problem is that nuclear weapons are all around us. Nearly every country has them even if they don't openly admit it. Worse yet is the fact that anyone can easily build a bomb from plans posted on various Internet websites. All you need is a small quantity of uranium which is supposedly easily available at many hospitals and pharmacies.

The danger posed by nuclear weapons is all too real and something must be done to combat this threat to the world. I propose the following solution.

First, we must collect and destroy all nuclear weapons and sources of radiation. We need someone like the UN to collect all of the missiles and bombs and destroy them once and for all.

Then, we must erase all knowledge about building nuclear bombs. Since man cannot be trusted with this knowledge we need to destroy all plans and instructions on building bombs. While science is important this is one area of knowledge that it can do without. Once all plans and documents relating to nuclear bombs are destroyed it will take centuries for man to relearn how to build them.

These two simple but decisive steps could rid the world of the threat of nuclear destruction. Once and for all we could all sleep at night without the fear of a nuclear nightmare.

Why This Essay Bombed

The problem with this essay is that the writer clearly does not have any knowledge about nuclear proliferation. Not only do some of the facts cited seem to have come from urban legends but there is no mention of the international aspect or diplomatic dimension of the issue. The second weak point of the essay is the solution—it is entirely unrealistic.

How do we go about collecting weapons? Is it even possible to remove knowledge once it is known? The writer assumes these are easy solutions when in fact they are extremely difficult, if not impossible.

How to Avoid This Mistake

Don't write about an issue without understanding it. You don't have to be an expert, but you should read about it and even discuss it with some teachers or professors. By speaking about the issues with others, you will gain a better understanding of a problem and this will also help you to generate innovative solutions. Your suggestions do not have to be easy or even doable, but they do need to show some thought and understanding of the difficulty involved in solving any large national or international problem.

If possible, draw a connection between the issue and your own life. Have you taken action even on a personal level? Remember that the scholarship judges don't want a lecture on the issue as much as they want to learn about you and your ability to analyze a complex problem.

CHAPTER SEVEN

JUDGES' ROUNDTABLE:
THE SCHOLARSHIP ESSAY

In this chapter:

- **Why the scholarship essay is so important**

- **Common qualities of money-winning essays**

- **How to avoid essay mistakes**

Meet the Scholarship Judges

In this second roundtable, judges and experts provide insight into the importance of scholarship essays and the qualities of those that win.

Q How important is the essay to winning a scholarship?

For many scholarship competitions the essay plays a vital role. It allows the selection committee to get to know you beyond a list of courses and achievements. In some competitions, the essay alone is the deciding factor that separates those who receive awards from those who don't.

Kimberly Hall
United Negro College Fund
"The essay is a very important piece of the application because it is often what the donor, who makes the final decision, will use to see the student's aspirations. It gives us a sense of who the student is and what they want to do with the money. It gives us a more complete picture of the student as a whole person as opposed to just a name."

Jacqui Love Marshall
Knight Ridder Minority Scholars Program
"In the end if we had to look at a student who had a little lower score and a little lower GPA but wrote an outstanding essay from the heart and had some experience or testimonials to back up their strengths, we'd be inclined to award the student with the strong essay. What really differentiates one applicant from another is a genuinely written essay."

Q What qualities make an essay powerful?

One of the keys to writing a powerful scholarship essay is to be honest and to write from the heart. The scholarship judges and experts have stressed that they can see through an essay that is not honest and that the best essays are about something for which the applicants are truly passionate.

Georgina Salguero
Hispanic Heritage Youth Awards
"We look at how you develop your thesis statement. What are you going to talk about and do you stick to those points? Do your paragraph structures make sense? We can tell how passionate you are for your subject by how you write. Don't just write that you want to attend college because you know you have to go to school. Instead, tell us why. Why do you want to go to college? What drives you? What gives you the strength to keep going?"

Shirley Kennedy Keller
American Association of School Administrators
"It's very important for them to be specific, to give specific examples of their leadership, special talents, obstacles or community service. The more specific they can be and the more they can back up their statements, the better they're going to fare in the judging process."

Kimberly Hall
United Negro College Fund
"Essays should be well developed in terms of the paragraph structure. The essay should have a definite purpose and direction. By the end of the essay we should know where you have started from and where you are heading. We want to see what you have dealt with and what your plan of action is. We also want to see where you see yourself in the future."

Trisha Bazemore
Coca-Cola Scholars Foundation
"You can tell when you read an essay if it's a real expression of something the student really cares about or if it was written just to impress. We intentionally don't provide students with instructions for the essay. We want to give each student the opportunity to be genuine."

Jacqui Love Marshall
Knight Ridder Minority Scholars Program
"Your essay needs to fit the scholarship. Sometimes when reading an essay you get the feeling that the essay was written generically for 60 different scholarships and the author just substituted newspapering for engineering. If you want to win our scholarship your essay needs to tie into your involvement to the things we care about like the newspaper, photography or the sales or marketing side of the business."

Wanda Carroll
National Association of Secondary School Principals
"Go back to your basic English lessons and remember all that your English teacher taught. Make sure your essay is concise and there's a point to what you're writing."

Laura DiFiore
FreSch! Free Scholarship Search
"If you can make the reader laugh, cry or get angry, even when you're just writing about yourself, you've already won half the game. That's the bottom line. Get an emotional response out of the reader."

Q What common mistakes do students make on the essay?

As you're writing the essay, it's important to know what works. But sometimes it can be even more helpful to know what doesn't work. By knowing what mistakes kill an otherwise good essay you can avoid them in your own writing. After having read hundreds or even thousands of essays, our panel has encountered many common mistakes that students make in their scholarship essays.

Kimberly Hall
United Negro College Fund
"Some students write their essays about the difficulties that they have faced but do so in a negative way and don't explain how they've overcome the difficulties. I would recommend that students present a positive light. Here are some of the challenges that I've had to overcome and here is how I did it. Stay positive."

Tracey Wong Briggs
All-USA Academic Teams
"There are some students who have outstanding biographical information, but when you read the essay all they've done is recount the facts that are in their application form. We want you to use the essay to go deeper and beyond what is listed in your application. We lose very good nominees that way. They just don't give you a clear idea of who they are beyond the basic facts."

Mario A. De Anda
Hispanic Scholarship Fund
"One of the common mistakes is that they use the same personal statement for many scholarships. They even forget to change the name of the scholarship they are applying to. We encourage students to make sure they write a personal statement specifically for the program."

Laura DiFiore
FreSch! Free Scholarship Search
"A huge mistake is what I call the crush, when we're getting 40 to 50 percent of our applications in the last three days. I think a lot of students would be better off if they didn't apply in the last two weeks before the deadline. The ones rushing to get in by the deadline would probably be better off spending more time on their essays and applying next year."

Wanda Carroll
National Association of Secondary School Principals
"Spelling. You should use your computer's spell check. We wouldn't disqualify an applicant solely on spelling, but the committee does see the mistakes and it does distract from the quality of the essay. If they had a choice between two equally well-written essays, they would choose the essay without spelling errors."

Leah Carroll
U.C. Berkeley Haas Scholars Program
"The most common error I run into is people who are trying to say what the foundation wants to hear. It ends up sounding inauthentic. I tell students to write as if they are trying to explain something to a friend. Just write from the heart. They seem to always come out better that way. Another mistake is that students, at Berkeley in particular, often sell themselves short. You should not be afraid to call attention to all of your achievements."

Michael Darne
CollegeAnswer
"When approaching the essay a lot of students are eager to dump a huge laundry list of achievements—a list of everything that they've done. But what scholarship providers are looking for is to get an understanding of who this person is and where they're going in life. They don't just want a list of accomplishments. If you can paint some picture of yourself, where you're going and how you're going to get there, you're going to be in a much better situation."

Georgina Salguero
Hispanic Heritage Youth Awards
"We're not giving the award to the best sob story. We're not looking for someone who can write the best woe is me story. Please don't give us this kind of essay."

Participating Judges & Experts

Trisha Bazemore, Program Assistant, Coca-Cola Scholars Foundation

Tracey Wong Briggs, Coordinator, *USA Today* All-USA Academic and Teacher Teams

Leah Carroll, Coordinator, U.C. Berkeley Haas Scholars Program and former program coordinator, U.C. Berkeley Scholarship Connection

Wanda Carroll, Program Manager, National Association of Secondary School Principals

Michael Darne, Director of Business Development, CollegeAnswer.com, the website of Sallie Mae

Mario A. De Anda, Director of Scholarship Programs, Hispanic Scholarship Fund

Laura DiFiore, Founder, FreSch! Free Scholarship Search Let's Get Creative Short Story and Poetry Scholarship Contest

Kimberly Hall, Peer Program Manager, United Negro College Fund

Shirley Kennedy Keller, Program Director, American Association of School Administrators

Jacqui Love Marshall, Vice President of Human Resources, Diversity and Development, Knight Ridder Minority Scholars Program

Georgina Salguero, Senior Manager, Programs and Events, Hispanic Heritage Youth Awards

CHAPTER
EIGHT

WINNING INTERVIEW STRATEGIES

In this chapter:

- The two types of interviews

- How to ace the interview

- Who are the interviewers

- How to dress and act

- What to do if you have a disaster interview

Face-to-Face with the Interview

Let's start with some good news. If you are asked to do an interview for a scholarship competition it means that you are a serious contender. Most competitions only interview a small number of finalists who make it through the initial round based on their application and essay. The bad news is that you will now undergo the nerve-wracking scrutiny of an interview with one or more scholarship judges. If the thought of this makes your palms moisten or you get a sinking feeling in your stomach, you are not alone.

The best way to overcome a fear of the interview is to know exactly what to expect and to be prepared for the questions you might be asked. In this chapter, we discuss what scholarship interviewers are looking for in your answers, and we will share some strategies to help you prepare.

Many students wonder why they have to do an interview in the first place. While some scholarships are awarded solely based on the written application, many scholarship committees like to perform face-to-face interviews to make the final decision. Particularly, if the scholarship is for a significant amount of money, the selection committee wants to be sure to give it to the most deserving student.

Having sat on both sides of the interview table, we can attest to the fact that an interview can shed significant insight on an applicant. Before we discuss how to make the most of the interview, let's cover the two situations you may face.

Friendly & Hostile Interviews

There are basically two types of interviews: 1) friendly and 2) less than friendly or even hostile. The friendly interview is fairly straight forward with the scholarship judges asking easy to answer questions that will help them get to know you better. While most interviews fall into the friendly camp, others especially for highly competitive and prestigious awards such as the Rhodes or Truman are far less pleasant. In these interviews the scholarship judges want to test you to see how you react to stressful and difficult questions. A hostile interview creates an environment for the judges to be able to evaluate how you react to pressure.

Whenever you encounter hostile judges or interview situations, keep in mind that they are not trying to personally attack you or diminish your accomplishments. Rather, they are observing how you respond to the situation. It is really a test of your ability to deal with difficult questions. Also, keep in mind that they will act the same toward all applicants.

How to Ace the Interview

Regardless of the type of interview, the keys to success are the same.

First, remember that scholarship interviewers are real people. This is especially true for hostile situations in which you may have to fight feelings of anger or frustration with the interviewer. Your goal is to create as engaging a conversation as possible. This means you can't give short, one-sentence answers and you certainly should not be afraid to ask questions. Most interviewers enjoy conversations over interrogations.

The second key to the interview is to practice. The more you practice interviewing, the easier and more natural your answers will be. Practice can take the form of asking and answering your own questions out loud or finding someone to conduct a mock interview. Consider taping your mock interview so you can review your technique. Having someone simulate a hostile interview is very good practice and will give you a tremendous edge over applicants who have not experienced this yet.

Transform Any Interview from an Interrogation into a Conversation

The reason most people volunteer to be scholarship judges is because they are passionate about the organization or award they support. Being an interviewer is hard work. In most cases, interviewers have a few questions to begin with but then hope the interviewee can help carry the conversation and direct it into other interesting areas. In fact, it is very difficult to interview an applicant who quickly and succinctly answers the questions but offers nothing else to move the conversation forward.

As the interviewee you are an essential part of determining where the conversation goes and whether or not it is easy or difficult for the interviewer. Your job is to supply the interviewer not only with complete answers but also with information that leads to other interesting topics of conversation.

It helps to know something about the interviewers. One thing you know is that they care about their organization. They may be members of the organization or long-time supporters. The more you learn about the organization and its membership the better idea you'll have about the interviewers and what interests them.

This knowledge is useful in choosing how to answer questions that require you to highlight a specific area of your life or achievements. It will also give you a feel for topics to avoid and questions you should ask.

Before every interview, do homework on the award and the awarding organization, which includes knowing the following:

Purpose of the scholarship. What is the organization hoping to accomplish by awarding the scholarship? Whether it's promoting students to enter a certain career, encouraging a hobby or interest or rewarding students for leadership, every scholarship has a mission. By understanding why the organization is giving away the money, you can share with the interviewers how you meet their priorities.

Criteria for selecting the winner. Use the scholarship materials to get a reasonable idea of what the selection committee is looking for when choosing the winner. From the kinds of information they request in the application to the topic of the essay question, each piece is a clue about what is important to the scholarship committee.

Background of the awarding organization. Do a little digging on the organization itself. Check out its website or publications. Attend a meeting or speak with a member. From this detective work, you will get a better idea of who the organization's members are and what they are trying to achieve. Knowing something about the organization will also prevent you from making obvious blunders during the interview.

Advice from a Rhodes Scholar
Kristin N. Javaras, Oxford University

The interview is one of last hurdles to becoming a prestigious Rhodes Scholar. Kristin, who is working on a doctorate in statistics at Oxford University, says about interviews, "The best advice I can offer is to be yourself, as trite as that may sound."

But what happens when you are stumped for an answer? "If you just don't know the answer to a question, don't be afraid to admit it," advises Kristin.

Regarding the type of questions that she was asked, Kristin recalls, "Almost every question was at least tangentially and often directly related to topics and experiences mentioned in my personal statement or included in my list of activities and jobs."

Once you've done the detective work, think about how the information can help you. Let's take a look at an example piece of information. Imagine you discovered that the organization offering the scholarship values leadership. In addition, you discover from reading the organization's website that all of its members are invited to join only if they have led large companies. Knowing this you could guess that the interviewers will probably be business leaders and will be most impressed if you highlight leadership and entrepreneurial activities. If asked about your greatest achievement you can insightfully highlight being president of your school's business club over anything else.

Knowing something about the interviewers beforehand will also help you think of appropriate and engaging questions. Most interviewers allow time to ask a few questions toward the end of the interview. By asking intelligent questions (i.e., not the ones that can be answered by simply reading the group's website), you will hopefully be able to touch upon something the interviewer really cares about that will lead to further conversation.

Going back to the example, you might ask a question such as, "As the president of the business club one of my greatest challenges has been to get funding from businesses for new projects and ideas. What advice do you have for young business people to secure seed money from established businesses?"

This question not only demonstrates that you know the background of the interviewers but also poses a question that they can answer with their expertise, and it could start a new conversation about how to fund a business idea.

You Are Not the Center of the Universe

Despite what you think, you are not the center of the universe—at least not yet! Therefore, in the interview you need to keep it interactive by not just focusing on yourself.

This can be accomplished by asking questions and engaging in two-way conversation. If you don't ask any questions, it will appear that you are not attentive or that you haven't put much thought into the interview. Beforehand, develop a list of questions you may want to ask. Of course you don't have to ask all of the questions, but be prepared to ask a few.

To get you started, we've developed some suggestions. Adapt these questions to the specific scholarship you are applying for, and personalize them.

- How did you get involved with this organization?
- How did you enter this field? What was your motivation for entering this field?
- Who were your mentors? Heroes?
- What do you think are the most exciting things about this field?
- What professional advice do you have?
- What do you see as the greatest challenges?
- What do you think will be the greatest advancements in the next 10 years?
- What effect do you think technology will have on this field?

The Group Interview
Key Strategies

So it's you on one side of the table and a panel of six on the other side. It's certainly not the most natural way to have a conversation. How do you stay calm when you are interviewed by a council of judges? Here's how:

Think of the group as individuals. Instead of thinking it's you versus the team, think of each of the interviewers as an individual. Try to connect with each separately.

Try to get everyone's name if you can. Have a piece of paper to jot down everyone's name and role so that you can refer to them in the conversation and be able to target your answers to appeal to each of the constituents. For example, if you are interviewing with a panel of employees from a company and you know that Sue works in accounting while Joe works in human resources, you can speak about your analytical skills to appeal to Sue and your people skills to appeal to Joe.

Make eye contact. Look into the eyes of each of the panelists. Don't stare, but show them that you are confident. Be careful not to focus on only one or two panelists.

Respect the hierarchy. You may find that there is a leader in the group like the scholarship chair or the CEO of the company. Pay a little more attention to stroke the ego of the head. A little kissing up never hurt anyone.

Try to include everyone. In any group situation, there are usually one or two more vocal members who take the lead. Don't focus all of your attention only on the loud ones. Spread your attention as evenly as possible.

Ultimately, the more interaction you have and the more you engage the interviewers the better their impression of you. You want to leave them with the feeling that you are a polite and intelligent person who is as interested in what they have to say as in what you do yourself.

Dress & Act the Part

Studies have shown than in speeches, the audience remembers what you look like and how you sound more than what you actually say. While it may seem unimportant, presentation style and presence are probably more significant than you think.

Think about the delivery of your answers and keep the following points in mind:

Sit up straight. During interviews, don't slouch. Sitting up straight with your shoulders back conveys confidence, strength and intelligence. It communicates that you are interested in the conversation.

Speak in a positive tone of voice. One thing that keeps interviewers engaged is your tone. Make sure to speak with positive inflection in your words. Convey confidence in your answers by speaking loudly enough for the judges to hear you clearly. This will not only maintain your interviewers' interest but will also suggest that you have an optimistic outlook toward life.

Don't be monotonous. Speaking at the same rate and tone of voice without variation is a good way to give the interviewers very heavy eyelids. Record yourself and pay attention to your tone of voice. There should be a natural variation in your timbre.

Speak at a natural pace. If you're like most people, the more nervous you are the faster you speak. Combat this by speaking on the slower side of your natural pace. During the interview you might think that you are speaking too slowly, but in reality you are probably speaking at just the right pace.

Make natural gestures. Let your hands and face convey action and emotions. Use them as tools to illustrate anecdotes and punctuate important points.

Make eye contact. Eye contact engages interviewers and conveys self-assurance and honesty. If it is a group interview, make eye contact with all of the interviewers—don't just focus on one. Maintaining good eye contact can be difficult, but just imagine little dollar signs in your interviewers' eyes and you shouldn't have any trouble. Ka-ching!

What It's Like to Be an Interviewer
Behind the Scenes with the Selection Committee

Selection committees are typically composed of volunteers who sign up for a long day of interviews. By understanding their role, you can see the importance of interacting with them, keeping their attention and giving them a reason to want to listen to what you have to say.

Each year the selection committee for this international service organization in the San Francisco Bay Area interviews about 15 applicants. The six or seven selection committee members, club members and previous scholarship winners, start the day at 8:30 a.m. and end at 6 p.m., with 45 minutes for lunch and a couple of stretch breaks. They spend about 30 minutes with each applicant.

"After the interview, we score and go to the next one," says Russ Hobbs, district scholarship chairman.

Surprisingly, Hobbs says there is no advantage to interviewing earlier in the day than later. Still, to be fair, they schedule the interviews randomly instead of alphabetically. Despite the long day Rotary has little trouble finding volunteers, he says, "Because the applicants are such phenomenally interesting people."

Smile. There's nothing more depressing than having a conversation with someone who never smiles. Don't smile nonstop, but show some teeth at least once in a while.

Dress appropriately. This means business attire. No-no's include: caps, bare midriffs, short skirts or shorts, open-toe shoes and wrinkles. Think about covering obtrusive tattoos or removing extra ear/nose/tongue/eyebrow rings. Don't dress so formally that you feel uncomfortable, but dress nicely. It may not seem fair, but your dress will affect the impression you make and influence the judgment of the committee.

By using these tips, you will have a flawless look and sound to match what you're saying. All of these attributes together create a powerful portrait of who you are. Remember that not all of these things come naturally, so you'll need to practice before they become unconscious actions.

How to Make Practice into Perfect

The best way to prepare for an interview is to do a dress rehearsal before the real thing. This allows you to run through answering questions you might be asked, practice honing your demeanor and feel more comfortable when it comes time for the actual interview. Force yourself to set aside some time to run through a practice session at least once. Here's how:

Find mock interviewers. Bribe or coerce a friend or family member to be a mock interviewer. Parents, teachers or professors make great interviewers.

Prep your mock interviewers. Give them questions (such as those in the next chapter) and also ask them to think of some of their own. Share with them what areas of your presentation you are trying to improve so that they can pay attention and give constructive feedback. For example, if you know that you fidget during the interview ask your interviewers to pay special attention to your posture and movements during the practice.

Capture yourself on video. Use a phone to video yourself so that you can review the mock interview. Position the phone behind your interviewer so you can observe how you appear from the right perspective.

Get feedback. After you are finished the practice interview, get constructive criticism from your mock interviewer. Find out what you did well and what you need to work on. What were the best parts of the interview? Which of your answers were strong, and which were weak? When did you capture or lose your interviewer's attention? Was your conversation one-way or two-way?

Review the video. Watch the video with your mock interviewer for additional feedback. Listen carefully to how you answer questions to improve on them. Pay attention to your tone of voice. Watch your body language to see what you communicate.

Do it again. If you have the time and your mock interviewer has the energy or you can find another person willing to help, do a second interview. If you can't find anyone, do it solo. Practice your answers, and focus on making some of the weaker ones more interesting.

The bottom line is this: the more you practice, the better you'll do.

The Long-Distance Interview

Interviewing over the telephone is a real challenge. While most interviews are held in person, sometimes you just can't meet face-to-face. When this happens, the telephone is the only option. The most difficult aspect of a long-distance interview is that you can't judge the reactions of the interviewers. You have no idea if what you are saying is making them smile or frown. While there is no way to overcome the inherent disadvantage of a phone interview, here are some tips that should help to bridge the distance:

Find a quiet place. Do the interview in a place where you won't be interrupted. You need to be able to pay full attention to the conversation.

The Hostile Interview
U.C. Berkeley & Truman Scholarship Winners

In some scholarship competitions, particularly ones for prestigious awards like the Rhodes, Marshall or Truman, the interviews are designed to challenge you. To do well you need to prepare and have the right mindset for these provocative interviews. —Gen and Kelly

During his interview to become a Truman Scholar, one of the eight panelists asked Brian C. Babcock to name a good funny novel he had recently read. Brian hadn't read a humorous novel recently, but he did have a children's book that he thought was funny.

He started to say, "It's not a novel, but..." and before he finished the interviewer interrupted him to say, "No, I want a novel."

The sentiment in most scholarship interviews is friendly and cordial. But for some competitions, particularly the prestigious ones with fierce national competition, the setting is often challenging and even adversarial.

"There's a kind of devil's advocate interviewing style for these competitions. The phrasing and tone is more antagonistic," says Leah Carroll, coordinator of U.C. Berkeley's Haas Scholars Program and former program coordinator of the university's Scholarship Connection office, which assists students who are applying for awards.

She coaches students to view these kinds of interviews as "intellectual sparring," and advises them to "practice interviews with friends and to tell their friends to be mean."

Donald H. Matsuda, Jr. experienced this intellectual sparring first hand. A student at Stanford University, Matsuda is also a Truman Scholar. The panel challenged his policy plan on health care for children asking why they should "continue to waste millions of our federal budget to help this situation that has no clear cut solution."

Brian's contributions reflect his own opinions, not those of the U.S. military.

Donald was also asked to define music. The panel gave him the option of defining it or singing a definition. He chose to define it. He said, "I see music as the ultimate way a person can express himself. I chose not to sing, which is why I think I won the Truman."

A student at the U.S. Military Academy, Brian applied for the award to receive a master's in foreign service and history and certificate in Russian area studies. In his interview, the selection committee asked Brian questions about gays in the Boy Scouts, an example of bad leadership and why he wanted to work in public service instead of make millions of dollars.

They challenged his choice of topic for his essay, asking why he chose as an example of leadership when he led one other person instead of when he led many. He answered, "If you can't lead one person how can you expect to lead a group?"

And, they questioned his grades, which weren't perfect but still high. He says, "I explained that to me it was more important to get the breadth of knowledge and take the classes while I have the time and it's free. I take as much as I can handle. If that means that my grades slip from a 3.9 to a 3.75 so be it."

Besides preparing for the interview, what may have helped Brian was his frame of mind. He says, "I didn't have an interview. I had a talk with eight people around the table."

Know who's on the other end of the line. You may interview with a panel of people. Write down each of their names and positions when they first introduce themselves to you. They will be impressed when you are able to respond to them individually and thank each of them by name.

Use notes from the practice interviews. One of the advantages of doing an interview over the telephone is that you can refer to notes. Take advantage of this.

Look and sound like you would in person. Pretend the interviewers are in the room with you, and use the same gestures and facial expressions that you would if you were meeting in person. It may sound strange, but the interviewers will actually be able to hear through your voice when you are smiling, when you are paying attention and when you are enthusiastic about what you're saying. Don't do the interview lying down in bed or slouched back in a recliner.

Don't use speaker phone, and have good reception for cell phones. Speaker phone often echoes and picks up distracting noise. If you have access to one, a land line is best, but if you use a cell phone, make sure the reception is strong.

Turn off call waiting. Nothing is more annoying than hearing the call waiting beep while you are trying to focus and deliver an important thought. (And, this may sound obvious, but don't click over to take a second call during the interview.)

The Disaster Interview

Even after doing interview homework and diligently practicing mock interviews, you may still find that you and the interviewer just don't connect or that you just don't seem to have the right answers. If you spend some time preparing, this is very unlikely. Interviewers are not trying to trick you or make you feel bad. They are simply trying to find out more about you and your fit with the award. Still, if you think that you've bombed, here are some things to keep in mind:

Avoid "should have," "would have," "could have." Don't replay the interview in your head again and again, thinking of all the things you "should have" said. It's too easy to look back and have the best answers. Instead, use what you've learned to avoid making the same mistakes in the next interview.

There are no right answers. Remember that in reality there are no right answers. Your answers may have not been perfect, but that doesn't mean they were wrong. There are countless ways to answer the same question.

The toughest judge is you. Realize that you are your own greatest critic. While you may think that you completely bombed an interview, the interviewer will most likely not have as harsh an opinion.

Post-Interview

After you complete the interviews, follow up with a thank you note. Remember that interviewers are typically volunteers and have made the time to meet with you. If you feel that there is very important information that you forgot to share in the interview, mention it briefly in a thank you note. If not, a simple thank you will suffice.

Make Sure You Make Your Point
Jason Morimoto, State Farm Exceptional Student

"I have been involved in practically every type of interview whether it be a single interviewer, a panel or a phone interview.

"The toughest by far are the phone interviews because the scholarship committee cannot physically see who you are and your facial expressions.

"I personally prefer the panel interviews because it gives you a chance to make a strong impression on multiple people. I have found great success with panels.

"However, no matter what the format of the interview, the most important thing is to make sure that you get across your main strengths. If they do not ask you directly, try to weave it in with a related story or tie it in as a closing statement. You always want to give the most information possible to the interviewers so that they can understand your uniqueness as a person."

CHAPTER
NINE

REAL INTERVIEW QUESTIONS & ANSWERS

In this chapter:

■ **See what makes a great answer**

■ **Questions you'll likely face in the scholarship interview**

■ **Interview tips from winners**

Giving the Right Answers

Imagine that your professor gave you the questions to an exam before you took it. Your score would certainly be higher. In this chapter we give you precisely this advantage by sharing the questions you're likely to be asked in scholarship interviews. Plus, we show examples of how to answer. You will be a fly on the wall, observing a typical scholarship interview.

Before the preview, we have a couple of caveats. Remember that these questions and answers are meant to be examples. Each of these is not the only acceptable way to answer a question. In fact, there are innumerable ways to answer each question successfully.

Also, since your background and achievements are different, your answers will inevitably be different too. Don't focus on the specific details of the answers. Instead, look at the overall message and impression that each answer conveys.

The comments that follow each question are based on interviews with actual scholarship judges as well as our own experience in competing for scholarships. To get the most out of this chapter, we suggest that you read a question first. Pause to think about how you would answer it. Then read the response and comments. Keeping the comments in mind, analyze how the judges might react to your response. Be tough on yourself and think of ways to strengthen your answers. If your parents or friends are helping you practice interviewing, ask them to read through a couple of the questions and answers to get a better idea of what kind of questions to ask and what to look for in responses.

Achievements & Leadership Questions

Q: **What achievement are you the most proud of?**

A: This may not seem like an achievement to many people, but it is for me. Last year I learned how to swim. Ever since I can remember I've had a grave fear of the water. Anything above knee level was a frightening experience. Last year my little brother fell into a pool and had to be rescued by the lifeguard. As I stood by not able to help, I realized that I needed to learn to swim. Twice a week I went to swimming lessons. It was kind of embarrassing to be in a swimming class with elementary school students but I was determined to learn. It took an entire class for me to feel comfortable walking in the water up to my neck, but after eight weeks of lessons, I could actually swim several laps. I never thought that I could learn. I'm proud of this accomplishment not because it was difficult to learn but because of the huge fear I had to face and overcome to learn it.

A: Unlike other schools, ours never had a debate team. Because I plan to be an attorney, I wanted to get practice in debating so I decided to form a team. None of the teachers at my school had the time to be the faculty adviser so I contacted local attorneys. I finally found one who despite her busy schedule volunteered to help us. I recruited 12 other students to join and became the team captain. In our first year we made it to the district competition and won several rounds. For me this was my biggest accomplishment especially since now we have a core group of debaters who will continue the team after I graduate.

Comments

This is a challenging question because in addition to selecting and describing an accomplishment, you need to put it into context and explain its significance. The first answer vividly illustrates how this student overcomes his fears to learn how to swim. Everyone has something that he or she is deathly afraid of, and it is likely that the judges can easily relate to this accomplishment. Notice how the answer reveals why the student decided to face his fear of swimming and gives enough detail to create a mental picture. There is also a nice element of humor in the story that makes you smile.

The second answer is an excellent example of how to highlight an impressive achievement. While the scholarship judges may notice that this student is the founder of her school's debate team in the application, this answer underscores just how difficult it was to start the team. It also reveals the student's desire to be an attorney. The applicant ends nicely by emphasizing how her achievement has affected others and will continue to make a positive impact on the lives of her fellow students.

Q: How have you been a leader or displayed leadership?

A: I am the chair of my dorm committee, which consists of six officers. My job is to oversee the committee as well as 500 student residents. My responsibilities include planning the orientation for new students, organizing social activities and directing our dorm's annual charity event. It's a challenge to get students motivated for a special event because there are so many other ways that they can spend their time. I am most proud of the way that I have been able to mobilize the students in our dorm to support our annual charity event, the bowl-a-thon for lung cancer research. To make this event a success I knew that I needed the help of others in our dorm. I recruited and trained hall representatives to personally contact all 500 students in our dorm and encourage them to participate in the bowl-a-thon. In the end over 50 percent of the students participated. We had a higher participation rate and donation level than any other dorm at our school.

A: This year I organized an event to collect toys for underprivileged children. I started by writing an article for the school newspaper to raise awareness and to get students to donate toys. I had volunteers who also went to local businesses and asked for donations as well as a group that decided which families in our town would receive the toys. The toy drive was a huge success. We were able to provide toys to over 200 families and we solicited donations from over 50 local businesses.

Comments

What's notable about both of these answers is that the applicants don't just list off a bunch of titles and positions. Instead the students focus on one specific leadership position or activity and give enough detail to show the depth of their commitment. Citing concrete accomplishments like getting half of the dorm to participate or giving toys to more than 200 families also helps judges to better gauge the significance of each achievement. The second answer illustrates that you don't have to hold an official title or elected position in order to show leadership. This applicant, who does not hold an elected position, is still able to

Tip #1 from a Scholarship Winner
Elisa Tatiana Juárez, Brown University

"Be proud of what you've done. Don't be falsely modest, but also make sure that you don't give the impression of being egotistical. The ability to talk positively about my accomplishments took me a long time to learn. I was afraid showing people what I've done would make me sound too conceited. Always remember that the judges want to know why they should pick you. Show them."

answer this question impressively by describing how she organized an event. You can certainly be a leader and motivator even if you don't have an official title.

Personal Questions

Q: What is your greatest strength and weakness?

A: One of my strengths is my ability to lead. For example, at my school we didn't have a recycling program. The janitors wouldn't pick up the paper for recycling because it wasn't in their contracts. I met with our principal to discuss the problem, but he said the school didn't have the budget to pay for a recycling program. So I started a program myself. I got donations to buy bins to put in each of the classrooms and went to each class to make a speech to get volunteers to collect the papers for recycling. Every month, I gathered the volunteers for a meeting to discuss any changes or problems.

One of my weaknesses is impatience. I get frustrated when I see a problem but nothing is happening to fix it. I like to see people working toward solutions. I got very frustrated when I first found out that there was no recycling program at my school and especially when the janitors said they wouldn't pick up the recycling even though I thought it didn't require that much extra work. But I guess it was this frustration that led me to do something about it.

A: My strength is in math. Ever since elementary school I have been talented in math. In school, when everyone else was struggling with algebra and geometry, I didn't have any trouble. I just imagined the problems in my head, visualizing the pyramids, spheres and cones. My math teacher even asked me to grade homework assignments. And I've represented our school each year for the county math competition.

My weakness is creative writing. I think because of the way that my mind works, it can be difficult to write creative essays. This is one of the reasons that I took a creative writing class last summer, and it really helped. The instructor had us pretend to be another person in the class and write from the other person's perspective. We also went outside and imagined being the grass, trees and sun. I never thought like that before and it's really opened up my mind to some new possibilities. This is one area that I know I need to work to improve.

Comments

It's easy to say that your strength is that you work hard. But what will really prove this to the judges is an example. Use an example to illustrate your strength so that the judges can see what you mean. It's not enough to say that your strength is leadership. How have you led? What kind of results have come from your leadership? Why do you do it? Both of these strength answers are good in giving complete examples. But more importantly they also help to contrast and balance the weakness. In the second response where the applicant admits to not being a skilled creative writer, this not only reveals an honest flaw but also gives him an opportunity to show what action he has taken to improve. There is nothing wrong with acknowledging a weakness, but it is very impressive to see that you are also taking steps to transform that weakness into a strength.

Misinterpreting the Judges
Silver Knight Scholarship Winner

It's tempting to try to read the judges during the scholarship interview. You might think that the longer the interview or the more involved the selection committee gets, the better your performance. Unfortunately, it's very hard to accurately interpret the thoughts of others. When she interviewed for the Silver Knight scholarship, Elisa Tatiana Juárez was scared. After all, the Silver Knight award is a highly competitive program and is given to only 14 of the top students in Miami-Dade County.

Elisa had been on the other side of the interview table before as an interviewer so she thought she had a good sense of how judges react when they are really interested in a candidate.

"I thought that you could tell what the judges think of you by their responses," she says.

In the interview, Elisa described the STARS (Students and Teachers Advocating Research Science) program that she started at the Miami Museum of Science to provide opportunities for minority and economically disadvantaged students in the sciences. During her interview, she was disappointed that the judges seemed too enthusiastic about her work to the point that she thought they were faking their level of interest.

"In my interview, they were too encouraging," she says. "My image was they thought, `Good luck, but try again next year.'"

Thankfully, her interpretation of their reactions was completely opposite from reality and she won the award.

Q: Who is a role model for you?

A: Oprah Winfrey. I admire Oprah not because of her wealth but because through sheer determination and hard work she has built one of the largest media companies in the country. I am inspired by people like Oprah who didn't inherit wealth or fame but who built it on their own by setting goals and working hard to achieve them. She is also motivating because she has chosen to do what she wanted, not necessarily what was seen as the most popular thing to do. For example, instead of making her media company about sex and violence, she's taken a different route to make it about the positive things in life. I also want to live my life by what I think is right, even if that is at odds with what the majority feel I should do.

A: My father is my role model. He has taught me to endure difficult times with resolve. I always knew that my father didn't make a lot of money at his job and that our family's finances were stretched. But I only recently learned how stretched our finances were. There were points where my parents weren't sure how they were going to pay the bills. But looking at my father, you would never detect the stress that he was under. He always made sure that we kids had everything that we needed. We didn't have the brightest or newest things, but we were always cared for. I remember one Christmas when I was 12. My friends received the newest "in" toys for Christmas while I received a wooden car and airplane that my father had made. I still have those toys and plan to give them to my kids someday. That is what I admire about my father and hope that in the face of adversity I too can be as calm and innovative as he is.

Comments

When judges ask this question, their intent is to learn something about you through your choice of whom you admire. If you just say that your role model is golfing superstar Tiger Woods but offer no explanation why, you aren't sharing much about yourself. The judges won't know if Tiger is your role model because he's a good golfer, a Stanford graduate or something else. Both of these answers give specific reasons why the applicants idolize these people, and both support their choice with concrete and memorable examples. No matter whom you choose as a hero, be sure to know enough about him or her to explain what specific quality you want to emulate. Also, know their shortcomings since you may be asked about that as a follow-up question.

Q: What is your favorite book?

A: *Les Miserables* by Victor Hugo. When we first were assigned this book to read, it was pretty daunting. But as I started reading, I couldn't put it down. I became consumed with the characters, feeling their emotions. The book took me through the low points of Jean Valjean's arrests and the high point of his final release. Throughout, the book made me think about the line between right and wrong and whether or not someone who was wrong in the past could make up for his or her mistakes to experience true freedom. It really made me think about the ethics I live by and about the mistakes I've made in the past. It also inspired me to be more forgiving of people with whom I've had disagreements.

A: *The Day Lincoln Was Shot* by Jim Bishop. This book chronicles the last 24 hours of Lincoln's life from the perspective of the assassins and the government officials who were the target of the assassination plot. I normally don't get drawn into history books, but this one was an exception because the detail allowed me to imagine everything that was happening and I felt like I was actually there. After reading the book, I took a drive to Washington, D.C., to see the Ford Theater and the boarding house where Lincoln died. I could almost see Booth approaching the President from behind and the doctors working on the President in vain. This book brought history alive for me, and I have a whole new interest in the American presidency.

Comments

Neither of these answers are book reports—which is good since the judges are not asking for a summary of the book. What the judges want to learn is who you are through your selection of a book and why you say reading the book is important. Both of these answers show

how the book affected the reader. When thinking about which book to choose, ask yourself if your selection made you think differently or compelled you to take action. Ask yourself what specifically made you relate to a character. Also, don't feel that you have to select a classic. It's fine to say that your favorite book is *Charlotte's Web* or *Green Eggs and Ham*. What's important is not your selection of the book but why it is meaningful to you.

Why You Deserve to Win Questions

Q: **Why do you think you deserve to win this scholarship?**

A: I believe that by giving this award you are trying to help students who show academic promise and who will contribute to the community. Since my first day of school, my parents have instilled in me a commitment to academics, and I have a nearly perfect academic record. I am on track to graduating with highest honors. I have also been contributing to my community for many years. I started a program to provide books for a local elementary school's library. By using funds from book fairs, I increased the number of books at the elementary school from 500 to 2,500. My commitment to learning and public service are two things that I believe in very strongly and I will continue to do so throughout my life.

A: This award is meant to assist students who are interested in business. I have been an entrepreneur since I was a kid and convinced my parents that I could organize a neighborhood-wide garage sale. We raised several hundred dollars that way. In school, I started a tutor-matching business. Students let me know what kind of help they needed, and I matched them to an appropriate tutor. Through ventures like these I've learned the value of marketing, building relationships and having a business plan. I'm planning on majoring in business and have a business internship lined up this summer. Ultimately I would like to be a professor at a business school so that I can continue to learn and pass on to others the knowledge and skills that will make them successful in business.

Comments

Both of these applicants do a good job of focusing on the purpose of the award to clearly explain how their background and achievements fulfill this purpose. It's important to address how you meet the mission of the award or the awarding organization. Be as specific as possible. Don't just say that you should win the scholarship because you are a good student. Give details and examples to support what you say.

Q: What would winning this scholarship mean to you?

A: For me, winning this scholarship could mean the difference between going to college or working full-time. Without this award, I will need to work for a couple years to save up enough money to go to college. I've been accepted to the college that I want to attend, but I simply don't have the money to pay for it. My parents didn't go to college, and I'll be the first in my family. And I will go. The question is whether it will be now or in a couple years.

A: My parents have spent the last 17 years taking care of me. Now I have a chance to do something to help them by winning scholarships. I feel that I owe it to my parents to try as best I can to help pay for my education. Winning this award would help to reduce their burden and help me to fulfill my goal of repaying my parents for all that they have done for me.

A: While I plan to work during the school year to earn money, winning this scholarship would mean that I could work fewer hours. Instead of working 20 hours a week, I could work only 10 hours and spend my extra time on my studies. It's been tough to balance working with my studies, and winning this award would help immensely.

Comments

Impact is important. Scholarship committees are trying to get the maximum benefit from their award. If the award will make the difference between your being able to attend a college or not, say so. The judges will understand that this award is more meaningful to you than to a student who already has a way to pay for his or her education. But be careful not to unload all of the challenges you face in the form of a sob story. Remember that many of the other applicants also have financial needs.

Education & College Questions

Q: Why is education important to you?

A: I want a job that makes me personally satisfied and my dream is to work in the medical field. An important part of this is being able to help people on a daily basis. I also know that I need to be challenged to be happy. So the medical profession is a perfect match since it allows me to contribute to society while working in an intellectually challenging environment. This past summer I volunteered at our county hospital and worked closely with a neurologist. It intrigued me that he was able to look at a set of symptoms and test results and figure out what was wrong with someone. It was like being a detective except that solving the mystery meant helping a person get better. But I also know that my ability as a doctor will depend on how well I am educated. I know that for some students going to college is about getting grades and a general education. But for me it's not only about learning because in the future someone's life may depend on how much I learned.

A: To me, education represents a limitless future. At this point in my life, I can be anything. I can be a doctor, teacher, computer programmer or artist. There are a thousand different directions I could go, but the only way to get anywhere is through education. I am studying English with a minor in music. In my classes, I have done a variety of things from writing a research paper on the role of women writers to composing an original piece performed by my school's orchestra. This is what education is all about: exploring interests and discovering what really excites you. So I guess what education really means to me is the chance to find out who I am by being able to try, succeed and sometimes even fail.

Tip #2 from a Scholarship Winner
Brian C. Babcock, U.S. Military Academy

"One of the best things that I did was do a couple of practice interviews. The way we did it was that all of the Truman applicants at my school would meet over lunch with an expert on a topic and talk about it. For example, we'd have someone come in and we'd discuss the 'don't ask don't tell policy.' We were able to get the former drug czar to sit down and talk to us for an hour and a half about the drug policy. Not a bad person to speak with about the drug policy.

"My advice is to go into the interview thinking that you're just going to have a very fun discussion. I didn't have an interview. I had a talk with eight people around the table. They asked me difficult questions but it wasn't hostile."

Brian's contributions reflect his own opinions, not those of the U.S. military.

Comments

Both of these students make personal what could otherwise be a very general answer. Instead of recounting the history of education or statistics from the latest national survey on education, these students reveal how education has personally affected them. When you are answering this question ask yourself: What have you gained personally from education or what do you hope to gain? What benefits have you received from the educational system? Try to be specific. It's not enough to say that you value education. Who doesn't? Try to get to the root of why education is important. Give specific examples so that the judges will understand your personal reason for pursuing a degree.

Q: **What has influenced you to get a college education?**

A: I am the first person from my family to attend college. My parents immigrated to the U.S. when I was a child. Without a college education my parents turned to what they knew, which was running a restaurant. I have also had to work in the family restaurant since I was a child so I know how difficult the work is. They said that their dream was for me to go to college so that I would have a wide choice of careers. They don't regret their decision coming to the U.S. because they expect me to go to college and succeed. Attending college means that I will have opportunities that my parents never had and that I will reach not only my goals but the goals of my parents as well. They have sacrificed their lives for me to have a better one. I don't plan on letting them down.

A: Since most of the students from my high school go to college, this seems like a strange question since it was almost assumed by my parents, teachers and friends that college was the next step after graduating. But, I look at going to college as my chance to pursue what I love—which is to design and build robots. I don't know what the job market is for "robot builders" but I intend to find out, and the first step is to get a solid education. I am choosing which schools to apply to based on whether or not they offer classes in robotics. College represents the first step in my ultimate goal of merging what I love to do with a career.

Comments

Both of these answers go beyond what's expected. Almost everyone can say that they want to go to college because they think education is important. What makes these answers strong is that they are specific to the individual. Try to personalize your answer by explaining why you have been inspired to get a college degree. What specific incident or person motivated you? What do you hope to gain? Be as specific as possible to give the selection committee insight into what inspires you and to avoid relying on overused generalizations. Also, be sure to stay away from saying that you are going to college just to earn more moolah. On a practical level, earning a degree will enable you to earn more money, but you should focus on less-materialistic factors.

Q: Why did you choose your college?

A: When I was researching colleges, I figured out that I had three priorities. First, I wanted a college with a strong program in biology and opportunities for doing hands-on research as an undergraduate. This was important because I plan to become a researcher after graduating and want to get useful experience during my college years. Second, I wanted to attend a school in which classes were taught by professors and not graduate students. I learn best when I am inspired, and I knew that I would be best inspired by learning directly from professors who are shaping the field of biology. My third priority was to attend a school with diversity. I think that college is a place not only for book learning but for personal learning as well. It's my chance to meet people with different ideas and from different backgrounds.

Comments

This is an excellent example of how to reveal something about yourself through your answer. You don't want to be a tour guide, describing the well-known assets of the college. Explain why the college's features are important to you. Instead of saying that you chose the college because of its research facilities, explain how you plan to make use of the facilities. The more details and specifics you can give the better. If appropriate, walk the judges through the thought process you went through when selecting the college. This will help them understand what is important to you and also show them how seriously you consider a college education.

Academic Questions

Q: **What is your favorite subject in school and why?**

A: I enjoy studying English because I like writing. When I write, I feel like I can be myself or I can be a totally different person. I can step into the shoes of someone in the past or be someone who I'm not—like an explorer in the Sahara. Writing lets me see through another person's eyes and forces me to experience what their life must be like. The most difficult thing I ever wrote was a short story that won an award from my school's literary magazine. Because the story was about a woman, the hardest part of writing it was that as a male, I had to completely reevaluate how I viewed my world through the eyes of a woman. I can tell you that I have a whole new understanding of what life might be like for the opposite sex.

A: My favorite subject is civics. Most people don't understand the way that our government works and why so many checks and balances have been put into place. It's a system that doesn't always produce the results that I'd like to see, but I am fascinated by our attempts to make a system that is as close to perfect as possible. I can see myself working in government in the future.

Comments

Both of these answers clearly explain the applicants' choices. It would be easy just to name a favorite subject and leave it at that. But the judges are trying to understand why you like what you like. When answering a question like this, give reasons or examples for your selection. Don't state the obvious. If you are asked why English is your favorite subject, give more than "Because I like it" or "Because I'm good at it." You can also use a question like this as an opportunity to talk about an achievement or award. If you say that your favorite subject is English, you can speak about a writing competition that you won or the reading marathon that you started. This is a good springboard question which you can expand to bring your impressive achievements into the conversation.

Q: **Why did you select your major?**

A: I'm majoring in history. History is intriguing because there are so many ways to describe the same event. A good example is the Second World War. There are many different viewpoints depending on which country the writer is from, whether he was in the military or a civilian or at what level in the leadership chain he was. It's the historian's job to present the information in the most objective way possible while still understanding that there are a lot of subjective elements to history. To me it's like unraveling a mystery, except that the mystery is real.

Tip #3 from a Scholarship Winner
Emanuel Pleitez, Stanford University

"Be confident. Confidence is going to help you out in immeasurable ways. Some people think the interviewer is there just to ask questions and make you falter. Usually the interviewers are really nice and they want to get to know you. As long as you let the interviewer know what you're really about, you'll be fine. Smile and let the interviewer get to know you. To do this all you really need is confidence."

A: My major is sociology. I hadn't planned to study sociology, but in my first year I took a class on women and the law. We covered the history and effect of laws on women including laws covering maternity leave, pornography and employment. It was an eye-opening class in which we got to interact with women who had been personally affected by these laws. I was hooked. One of my most recent research papers is based on a survey of working-class women. I really care about this field and can relate to it in a personal way.

Comments

Both answers share the applicants' inspiration for selecting their majors. Try to bring the judges into your mind so that they understand why you are passionate about your field. Examples also help the judges, who may have no idea what your major is about, understand why you chose the field. Bring up some interesting facts about the major or hot issues in the field. You might try to also think about how the degree will help you after graduation. What effect on your future might your choice have? What are your plans for using the degree in the future?

Q: **Which educator has had the most influence on you?**

A: Without a doubt my economics professor. In his lectures he made the theories come to life by showing real life examples of how they worked. He also took the time to meet with each of us individually to get our feedback and to see if we were interested in majoring in economics. My meeting with him lasted for two hours. I explained that I was thinking about majoring in economics but I wasn't sure if I had the mathematical ability. He convinced me that I could work on my math skills as long as I had a passion for learning. I met with him several other times, and he agreed to be my thesis advisor. Of all my professors, he's the one who has made the most effort to make sure that I was learning and excited about the field.

A: I had a professor last year who taught design. He assigned us projects that I never imagined I'd be doing. At the start of class, he had a handful of toothpicks. He asked us, "What is this?" We all said matter-of-factly, "Toothpicks."

"No," he said. "It's a bridge."

So our assignment was to build a bridge that could support the weight of a bowling ball out of toothpicks. This professor taught me to look at everyday things in a different way, to notice the shape of a gate, the color of the sky after it rained or the shadow of a building on the ground. I learned to pause and appreciate all of the efforts that went into creating what's around me.

Comments

As much as possible try to illustrate the specific influence of a teacher or professor. Give concrete examples of what he or she has done to help you learn. This will give the judges insight into your learning style and what motivates you.

Be sure that you don't just select an educator who was cool, friendly or popular. If you had a teacher or professor with whom you shared a love for baseball but not for the subject matter, this is not a great choice. The judges want to learn about an educator who has inspired you to learn, not one who was a buddy.

Also, don't criticize other educators. In describing an influential teacher or professor, it is tempting to point out the negative traits of the others. Try not to do this. In many cases, the judges will be educators themselves or will be well-connected with educators. It would be a mistake to insult the profession. Focus on the positive aspects of the educator you choose.

Q: Can you tell me about an academic class, project or other experience that was meaningful for you?

A: One of the most meaningful projects I did was in my English class. We were assigned to develop a plan for the future of our local community. The problem was that the local agriculture industry was deteriorating and within the next five years would leave hundreds in our small community jobless and farmland without a use. We were assigned to create a five-year development plan. We planned the growth of our town, training programs for the displaced workers and redevelopment plans for the land. We each published a report and built a scale model of what the town would look like. Mine was one of the handful selected to be presented at a meeting of our city council.

A: For one of my sociology classes, I had to write a paper based on primary interviews. I knew that in order to be motivated to do the paper, I needed to write about something close to me. So I chose to write about the ethnic identities of first- and second-generation Asian American teenagers. Speaking with the teens, I learned how those in the first generation still had close ties to their home country while those in the second generation strived to just fit in with being American. It made me think about my own identity as a third-generation Asian American, and I started to ask questions of my own family. I could see that my family too went through a similar experience. What began as a class assignment actually helped me learn more about my family history.

Comments

A question of this type is a great opportunity to show off an impressive project. Be sure to give a lot of detail and demonstrate why the project or class was so meaningful. If appropriate, select a subject or project that relates to the scholarship since it will help demonstrate why you deserve to win the award.

Your Career & Future Questions

Q: Why do you want to enter this career?

A: I want to be a journalist because I want people to react to my writing. Whether I am uncovering an injustice or celebrating a hero, I want to invoke readers to respond. I recently wrote an article on ethnic barriers on our college's campus—how students tend to socialize with others of the same ethnic background. That series of articles sparked a huge controversy on campus. The minority clubs asked me to be on a panel discussion on the topic. Over 300 students came. There were a lot of tense moments, but I think they were necessary. My article made people think about a tough subject.

A: It might sound like a cliché to say that I want to become a doctor because of a television show, but for me it's true. I became inspired after watching "Grey's Anatomy." I know that the show is a fictionalized drama with the purpose of entertaining and that it is as much about the personal lives of the doctors as the medicine that they practice. But what inspires me is seeing the characters act selflessly for the good of their patients. It's heartening to see that even though people see medical care as impersonal and bureaucratic, these characters give a human and humane face to the field. That's a trait that I think is important and that I want to carry with me when I become a doctor.

Tip #4 from a Scholarship Winner
Dalia Alcázar, U.C. Berkeley

"Sometimes you fill out an application, send it off and it was something you did at 3 a.m. Then you get called in for an interview and you have completely forgotten what you had written.

"Before every interview I made sure I knew about the organization, what I had written on my application and what I had written about for the essay. I needed to know what information they had about me. I also took in resumes and I always carried a portfolio with letters of recommendation, a personal profile, certificates and some examples of my writing."

Comments

When judges ask this kind of question, what they really want to know is what inspires you. They want to see that you have a rationale for entering a profession. Be sure to give a reason even if it is something as simple as being influenced by a TV show. Help the judges understand your inspiration by using lots of examples. They will not only comprehend why you want to work in the industry but also what motivates you in general.

Q: What are your career plans?

A: Eventually I would like to be the managing editor of a major newspaper. I know that I will need to start out working as a journalist for a small circulation paper and slowly move up to higher circulation newspapers. During an internship with a newspaper last summer, I had the opportunity to meet with the managing editor. She described a day in her life. What really struck me was the number of serious decisions she had to make and that every day was different. I don't want to be in a job where I do the same thing every day. I want a job that constantly makes me think and interact with a variety of people. I know it will take years of hard work and perseverance, but I think that I have the decision-making and management ability to do this kind of job well.

A: My goal is to start my own nonprofit organization to provide programs for inner-city youth. In high school and in college I have volunteered with groups to help underprivileged kids. It's been great to see how much of a difference a few hours a week can make in the life of a child. I'm a big sister to a sixth grade student now, and we've developed such a strong relationship that she asked me to go to her sixth grade graduation. I'd begin by working for a nonprofit organization. Eventually I'd like to start my own nonprofit group. I think I can help the most children this way.

Comments

Both of these applicants are aiming high, which is a very good thing. It's important to show the scholarship committee that you have high ambitions, will hold a leadership role in the future and that you are striving to make significant achievements in the career field. Explain how you would like your career to progress and what you would like to achieve. Remember that organizations awarding scholarships have limited funds and want their dollars to have the largest impact possible. This makes it important for scholarship committees to provide their awards to students who will make contributions to the field, who will be role models for others and who may directly participate in their organization in the future. Share with the selection committee what kind of influence you intend to make moving forward. Of course, you don't need to have your entire future planned out. But the scholarship judges do expect you to have a general idea of what you perceive is ahead of you.

Q Where do you see yourself 10 years from now?

A: I've asked myself that very question before and while nothing is set in stone, I do have a general idea of what I want to do and where I want to be in a decade. First, I plan to graduate from college with a degree in marketing that focuses on marketing communications. After college I'd like to work for a consumer products company to gain practical experience.

In 10 years, I'd like to take my big company experience and be a marketing manager at a smaller company, perhaps a start-up. I see myself working in marketing communications because I enjoy writing and I like the challenge of communicating complicated ideas to potential buyers. However, I think ultimately I would enjoy working in a smaller, more intimate environment, which is why I see myself at a smaller company after getting some experience. I also hope to have a family. My career will be important but not as important as my family.

A: I am majoring in political science. In 10 years, I'd like to run a nonprofit organization to help women gain equality in the workplace. Even though there have been gains for women with more females serving on executive boards and with increasing equity in pay, there is still a long way to go. Through the nonprofit organization, I'd like to provide training and recruitment programs to help women advance in business. I would also like to survey the track records of the representation of women at the executive level and lobby politicians to support women's issues.

A: In 10 years, I hope to be working for a clinic as a pediatrician. I believe that all children have the right to quality medical care whether their parents can afford it or not. Those who have lower incomes do not deserve second-class medical care. I'd like to be a part of eradicating that situation, working at a clinic and helping the children who need it the most. I would get more personal satisfaction from this than anything else.

Comments

The key to answering this question is acknowledging that the judges want to understand your motivation, not just the fact that you want to be CEO of a company. These students' responses demonstrate their inspiration. Judges also like to see the passion of students who still have their entire future ahead of them. Giving this answer with energy and enthusiasm is essential. Of course, it is possible to go too far and sound naïve. Ideally your answers should be a mix of a healthy dose of youthful idealism with a touch of adult reality.

Activity Questions

Q: **What activities are you involved in?**

For an award for student-athletes:

A: The main activities that I'm involved in are soccer, the academic decathlon and student government. I am the captain of the soccer team, which has won the county championship for the past three years. I plan to continue to play that sport in college. I'm also the co-captain of the academic decathlon team. For the first time in our school's history we've made it to the state level competition. While it was a team effort, my co-captain and I recruited a teacher to coach us and organized extra study sessions that I think made the difference. My participation in student government includes serving as the vice president of our school. During my tenure I have directed our school's international festival, canned food drive and election process.

For an award for writing:

A: My most important activity is writing for my school's literary magazine. One piece that I wrote received an award in a writing contest. After traveling to Italy, I decided to write a creative piece about how my life would have been different had my great-grandparents not immigrated to America. I explained what kind of relationship I would have had with my family, my education and my vocation. In my piece, I incorporated memories that my grandparents had of their home country.

Comments

Don't give a laundry list of activities. Instead of telling all 12 clubs that you are a member of, select a handful in which you've made significant contributions. This will be more meaningful to the selection committee and will better capture their attention. Be sure to also highlight activities that match the goal of the awards. If you are applying for a writing award, speak about your writing experience. If you are applying for an award in medicine, speak about your medical-related experience, studies or volunteer work. Make the activities relevant to the selection committee.

Q: How have you contributed to your community?

A: One of the ways that I have contributed to my community is volunteering over 200 hours at our local library for the children's reading program. Three times a week I go to the library after school to read stories to the children and lead them in arts and crafts activities related to the books. I do this because I think it's important to get kids excited about reading and to expose them to new ideas. The artwork gets them to interact with the material and to be creative. I know that the volunteer work that I'm doing is making a difference because parents tell me that their children have learned to enjoy reading more because of my efforts.

A: I have contributed to my community by being a voice for teenagers. Last year there was a series of articles about how teens felt like they were second-class consumers. When we go to a store, we are frequently followed around so that we don't shoplift or we are treated poorly because of our age. I thought that this kind of treatment was unnecessary and wanted to send a message to the stores that were the main culprits. I organized a protest in front of four of these stores, getting teens to carry picket signs. We got media coverage, and there was another article to follow up on the changes the stores made. We were able to get the owners of all four of the stores to sign pledges to treat teens fairly.

Comments

Show the judges how significant your contribution has been by describing the effects. How many people were affected? In what way? Have you been honored for your contributions? Contributing to your community can go beyond volunteering. Remember that there are other ways to play a role in your community such as being an advocate for a cause. Your efforts do not have to be part of a formal organization or club.

Opinion Questions

Q: What is the most important issue to you?

A: I have been personally affected by underage drinking. A friend of mine was killed in an accident caused by a drunk driver. The accident was devastating not only to her family but also to our entire school. Since that happened, I began volunteering for a group that provides rides for people who have been drinking. Even though the people I drive home are in terrible shape and I ask myself how they could let themselves go so far, I treat them well knowing that at least they had the sense to get a ride home instead of driving themselves. This issue is important to me because I know that my friend's death could have been prevented.

A: It's important to me that children are exposed to the arts. In our school district, funding was cut for the music program at the elementary schools. I volunteered after school to teach students how to play the flute and had 10 students I taught regularly. I believe that the arts encourage students to think creatively, to recognize that there are different ways of communicating and to appreciate the beauty of music. I was exposed to music when I was a child and I think it's important that I help pass on that experience to other children.

Comments

When you are identifying a problem, try to also suggest some solutions. It is even more significant if you have tried to be a part of the solution. Of course, be careful not to sound like a Miss America contestant. Don't proclaim that you are going to single-handedly end the world's problems. Be realistic about your role in affecting the issue.

Q: Is there anything else you want to add?

A: We spoke about the activities that I'm involved in, but there's an important one that I forgot to mention. I've been volunteering at the local art museum as a docent, and the

Tip #5 from a Scholarship Winner
Donald H. Matsuda, Jr., Stanford University

"I think the idea with the Truman Scholarship interview is that it's supposed to be somewhat controversial. You go into a room and there is a panel of eight people. They are all distinguished public servants who are trying to test your commitment to your views and get a sense of who you are beyond what you put on paper. You need to be psychologically and emotionally ready for this type of interview so that you won't be surprised."

experience has been great. In classes, I've studied modern art. Working at the museum, however, has given me the opportunity to share my appreciation and knowledge with tour groups every week. More than anything else this experience has solidified my desire to become an art curator in the future.

A: I would like to emphasize how committed I am to obtaining a degree and becoming a teacher. Given the purpose of your award, I think that my background including my work with the after-school program and the awards that I have won for working with children shows that I have fulfilled many of the goals of the award. After graduating, I plan to work as a teacher in my school district. I think it's important that everyone recognizes where they got their start so that they can help others in the same way. That's the only way to make improvements.

Comments

Don't be shy about bringing up something important that the judges didn't ask you about. If you've forgotten to speak about something or a topic never came up during the conversation, now is the time to say so. Use this question to bring up a strong point or two that wasn't discussed. The last impression you leave is often the strongest. If you think you've already left a strong impression, then you don't have to say anything. But if you think you need to reemphasize an important point, this is the time to make a final statement. Use this opportunity to make sure that you have made it clear why you deserve to win the award.

CHAPTER TEN

JUDGES' ROUNDTABLE:
THE INTERVIEW

In this chapter:

■ Get the inside story from real scholarship judges

■ See what the judges think are the keys to a great interview

■ Learn what mistakes students make in the interview

Meet the Scholarship Judges

This is the last of three roundtables in this book. In this roundtable, scholarship judges and experts provide insight into the importance of interviews and what you can do to ace them.

If applying for scholarships is like running a race, then the interview is the last lap, the last step toward winning or losing and oftentimes the most important. It is also what worries students the most. Unlike the essay which you can write in the safety of your bedroom, for the interview you actually have to sit across the table from live human beings who are watching and evaluating your every word.

The key to acing the interview is to know what to expect and then to practice. While you may never shed the butterflies in your stomach, you can calm them down. In this roundtable we ask scholarship judges and experts what they are looking for in the interview.

 How important is the interview in determining who wins the award?

Brent Drage
Rotary International Ambassadorial Scholarship Program
"I would say that the most important part of our process is the interviews. It's important because it allows the Rotarians to speak with the applicants, see what they're like and get an idea of how they would act if they go abroad."

Jacqui Love Marshall
Knight Ridder Minority Scholars Program
"The interview can make a pretty big difference when evaluating two candidates. The interview plays the largest role in the final selection since we use it to narrow down our eight semifinalists to the three finalists."

Q What are some typical questions that you ask?

Because scholarship committees have similar goals—to get to know you beyond the written application and to determine your fit with the award—they ask similar questions. Here are some actual questions you are likely to be asked.

Brent Drage
Rotary International Ambassadorial Scholarship Program
"We typically ask questions related to the autobiographical essay that the student has submitted. We ask applicants to expand on their thoughts and ideas in their essays. We also ask them how they plan on contributing to the world when they graduate. How are they planning on making an impact?"

Jacqui Love Marshall
Knight Ridder Minority Scholars Program
"Typical questions include: Tell me about what you know about the newspaper business. Why do you want to enter into this career? How do your parents feel about your decision to pursue a career in newspapering?"

Q From your experience what are qualities of a good interview?

While there is no single correct way to answer an interview question, there are certain qualities that help to make a good interview stand out in the minds of scholarship judges. It can be difficult to pinpoint what the qualities are, but our panel offers some guidance. Keep in mind that there are a limitless number of ways to have great interviews and these points are meant to provide guidance and a starting point. A good interview does not necessarily need to embody every one of these qualities.

Jacqui Love Marshall
Knight Ridder Minority Scholars Program
"I think being very honest and straightforward is important. We can tell when a student is genuinely interested and passionate about the newspaper business. It is very hard to fake this level of enthusiasm."

Q What common mistakes do students make in interviews?

Scholarship interviews are one place where it may seem like there's nowhere to hide and every misspoken word is magnified. In most cases, you are probably your harshest critic, noticing your errors more than the interviewers. But we found that there are some mistakes that judges notice more than others. Fortunately, these mistakes are all avoidable.

Russ Hobbs
Rotary International Ambassadorial Scholarship Program
"Not doing your homework on our organization is an easy mistake to avoid. We had one applicant who attended an Ivy League college and flew across the country for his interview. When the selection committee asked him what he knew about Rotary he didn't have a clue. He relied completely on the fact that he was an Ivy League graduate. It was like applying for a job at Microsoft without knowing what Microsoft does. This applicant figured all he had to do was show up and sign for the check."

Leah Carroll
U.C. Berkeley Haas Scholars Program
"When we advise Berkeley students who are about to go into a difficult interview we remind them that they have to see this as intellectual sparring. You need to be prepared for an interviewer to challenge your ideas. You need to be able to defend your views and even poke back. We tell our students to go in with the attitude that it's challenging but also fun. We have found that a lot of judges are most impressed when students

are willing to defend who they are and feel good about their beliefs. Not being ready to do this or not practicing for this kind of interview is a huge mistake."

Q How should students prepare for interviews?

While interviews can be stress-inducing, there is something you can do to combat the tension–prepare. Here is some guidance for getting ready for the main event.

Russ Hobbs
Rotary International Ambassadorial Scholarship Program
"There are certain things that you can do to prepare for the interview. The no-brainer is knowing a little bit about Rotary. The interview is not designed to be a test like do you know all the capitals in the U.S. We presuppose that everyone is smart. What we're more interested in is the applicants themselves. What do you believe in? What do you stand for? Those aren't things that you can bone up on. They're either part of who you are or not."

Georgina Salguero
Hispanic Heritage Youth Awards
"The interview is your 15 minutes of glory. This is not the time to be modest. You have bragging rights. Use this opportunity. Prepare for it and know what you want to say."

Poor Ways to Begin an Interview
Various Scholarship Judges

First impressions are priceless since you only get one shot to make them. The following is a collection of tips from scholarship judges on how to avoid making a bad first impression.

"When walking into the room don't appear timid or afraid. Stride in with confidence. We learn a lot about an applicant from the way he or she crosses the distance from the door to the chair."

"Drink some water right before the interview. When nervous your throat naturally dries out and you don't want the first words the judges hear to sound unnaturally hoarse."

"Don't forget to look at all members of the judging panel when you speak. Some applicants look only at the members sitting directly in front of them but forget to turn to address those on the sides."

"Don't get our names wrong. Since we interview with a panel of five judges we don't expect applicants to remember our names. It's better not to use our names in conversation if you can't remember them than to call everyone by the wrong name."

"Sit up straight and still. Don't slouch or fidget. It can be very distracting."

"Don't hold pens or paper in your hands. It's too easy to unconsciously play with these objects while talking."

"Smile when you first walk in even if you feel nervous."

Participating Judges & Experts

Leah Carroll, Coordinator, U.C. Berkeley Haas Scholars Program and former Program Coordinator, U.C. Berkeley Scholarship Connection

Brent Drage, Resource Development Assistant, Rotary International Ambassadorial Scholarship Program

Russ Hobbs, District Scholarship Chairman, Rotary International Ambassadorial Scholarship Program

Jacqui Love Marshall, Vice President of Human Resources, Diversity and Development, Knight Ridder Minority Scholars Program

Georgina Salguero, Senior Manager, Programs and Events, Hispanic Heritage Youth Awards

CHAPTER ELEVEN

FINAL THOUGHTS

In this chapter:

- A personal ending

- A special request

A Personal Ending

When you are just beginning the scholarship search it may seem like a daunting–if not downright impossible–task. But you need to keep in mind that the rewards of finding and applying for scholarships are substantial. Every student we interviewed recalled how that when starting it seemed like winning was a long shot. However, each student did apply and ultimately won.

In this book you have met students who have won tens of thousands of dollars in scholarship money. You no doubt have noticed they all have different backgrounds, achievements and aspirations. When applying, take the time to highlight your strengths. Show the scholarship judges why you deserve to win.

You can do it. And the fact that you have made your way to the end of this book shows not only your commitment to winning but also gives you a tremendous advantage. Now you know what it takes to write a powerful essay and deliver a knockout interview. You have been witness to success and failure and learned from both.

We wrote this book because we wish that we had known what we do now back when we were applying. Although we were successful, we also learned some hard lessons that we want you to avoid.

We would like to end with a personal story. When I (Kelly) was applying for scholarships I found one offered by my father's company. I was a junior in high school and didn't have any idea what it took to win a scholarship.

I thought that scholarships were based entirely on grades and test scores. Since I had good grades and high PSAT scores I thought I would win. I quickly filled out the application and wrote an essay. When it came time to interview I didn't even practice. I went in cold and "winged it." The whole time I assumed that I would win based on my academic achievements. In fact, I was so confident that I actually spent the rest of the summer waiting for the check to arrive.

But the check never came.

When I found out who won I was shocked. The student had lower grades and test scores than I did! Why did he win? How unfair!

That's when I realized that the scholarship committee was looking for more than good grades and test scores. The following year I spent time on my essay. I also practiced for the interview with a friend.

While I had spent much more time and effort this time I was rewarded when one day, out of the blue, an envelope arrived with a $2,500 check enclosed.

You can win a scholarship through your essay and interview. Even though you might be tempted like I was to bang out an essay and run into an interview cold, don't. You'll spend less time but you won't win.

It takes time and effort to craft a powerful essay and hone your interview skills. But there are a lot of awards out there and someone has to win. Let's make sure that it's you.

Special Request

Before you embark on your own quest for scholarships, we have a special request. We would love to hear about your experiences with scholarships. We want to know what works and what doesn't and how this book has helped you. Please send us a note after you've finished your own winning scholarship essays and interviews. You can reach us at:

Gen and Kelly Tanabe
c/o SuperCollege
2713 Newlands Avenue
Belmont, CA 94002

gen@supercollege.com
kelly@supercollege.com

$1,000 JumpStart Scholarship

College JumpStart Scholarship Fund
4546 B10 El Camino Real
No. 325
Los Altos, CA 94022
http://www.jumpstart-scholarship.net
Purpose: To recognize students who are committed to using education to better their life and that of their family and/or community.
Eligibility: Applicants must be 10th, 11th or 12th grade high school, college or adult students. Applicants may study any major and attend any college in the U.S. Applicants must be legal residents of the U.S. and complete the online application form including the required personal statement. The award may be used for tuition, room and board, books or any related educational expense.
Amount: $1,000.
Number of Awards: 3.
Deadline: April 15.
How to Apply: Applications are available online.

$1,000 Moolahspot Scholarship

MoolahSPOT
2713 Newlands Avenue
Belmont, CA 94002
http://www.moolahspot.com/index.cfm?scholarship=1
Purpose: To help students pay for college or graduate school.
Eligibility: Students must be at least 16 years or older and plan to attend or currently attend college or graduate school. Applicants may study any major or plan to enter any career field at any accredited college or graduate school. A short personal statement is required.
Amount: $1,000.
Number of Awards: Varies.
Deadline: December 31.
How to Apply: Applications are only available online.

$1,000 Plan for College Sweepstakes

Sallie Mae
300 Continental Drive
Newark, DE 19713
http://j.mp/sallie-mae-award
Purpose: To help students pay for college, Sallie Mae is awarding this $1,000 Plan for College Sweepstakes.
Eligibility: Enter to win $1,000 when you register for Sallie Mae's free college planning tools, resources, and calculators. It's fast, easy, free – and NO ESSAY required! No purchase necessary. Void where prohibited. Odds of winning depend on the number of entries received. See official rules for details.
Amount: $1,000.
Number of Awards: 1 per month.
Deadline: Monthly.
How to Apply: Applications are available online.

$1,000 Scholarship Detective Launch Scholarship

Scholarship Detective
http://www.scholarshipdetective.com/scholarship/index.cfm
Purpose: To help college and adult students pay for college or graduate school.
Eligibility: Applicants must be high school, college or graduate students (including adult students) who are U.S. citizens or permanent residents. Students may study any major. The funds may be used to attend an accredited U.S. institution for undergraduate or graduate education.
Amount: $1,000.
Number of Awards: 2.
Deadline: December 31.
How to Apply: Applications are available online.

AFSA National Essay Contest

American Foreign Service Association (AFSA)
2101 East Street NW
Washington, DC 20037
Phone: 202-944-5504
Fax: 202-338-6820
Email: dec@afsa.org
http://www.afsa.org
Purpose: To support students interested in writing an essay on foreign service.
Eligibility: Applicants must be U.S. Citizens, high school students and have parents who are not members of the Foreign Service. Students must attend a public, private, parochial school, home school or participate in a high school correspondence program in any of the 50 states, the District of Columbia or U.S. territories or must be U.S. citizens attending schools overseas. The current award is $2,500 to the student and an all expenses paid trip to Washington, DC, for the winner and parents.
Amount: $2,500.
Number of Awards: 1.
Deadline: March 15.
How to Apply: The registration form is available online. Applicants must write a 750- to 1,000-word essay on the topic provided.

Alpha Kappa Alpha Financial Need Scholars

Alpha Kappa Alpha Educational Advancement Foundation Inc.
5656 S. Stony Island Avenue
Chicago, IL 60637
Phone: 800-653-6528
Fax: 773-947-0277
Email: akaeaf@akaeaf.net
https://akaeaf.org/scholarships
Purpose: To assist undergraduate and graduate students who have overcome hardship to achieve educational goals.
Eligibility: Applicants must be studying full-time at the sophomore level or higher at an accredited institution and have a GPA of 2.5 or higher. Students must also demonstrate leadership, volunteer, civic or academic service. The program is open to students without regard to sex, race, creed, color, ethnicity, religion, sexual orientation or disability. Students do NOT need to be members of Alpha Kappa Alpha. Deadline is April 15 for undergraduate students and August 15 for graduate students.
Amount: Varies.
Number of Awards: Varies.
Deadline: April 15 and August 15.
How to Apply: Applications are available online. An application form, personal statement and three letters of recommendation are required.

American Bar Association Law Day Art Contest

American Bar Association (ABA)
321 North Clark Street
Chicago, IL 60654
Phone: 312-988-5000
http://www.americanbar.org
Purpose: To encourage students to learn about the legal system.
Eligibility: Applicants must be high school students in grades 9-12 or the equivalent within the United States. Students must create an art piece representing the theme for Law Day.
Amount: $750.
Number of Awards: 2.
Deadline: March 31.
How to Apply: Applications are available online.

American Fire Sprinkler Association High School Senior Scholarship Contest

American Fire Sprinkler Association
12750 Merit Drive
Suite 350
Dallas, TX 75251
Phone: 214-349-5965

Fax: 214-343-8898

Email: scholarship@firesprinkler.org

http://www.afsascholarship.org

Purpose: To provide financial aid to high school seniors and introduce them to the fire sprinkler industry.

Eligibility: Applicants must be high school seniors who plan to attend a U.S. college, university or certified trade school. Students must read the "Fire Sprinkler Essay" available online and then take an online quiz. Applicants receive one entry in the scholarship drawing for each question answered correctly.

Amount: $2,000.

Number of Awards: 10.

Scholarship may be renewable.

Deadline: April 1.

How to Apply: Applications are available online.

Americanism Essay Contest

Fleet Reserve Association (FRA)

FRA Scholarship Administrator

125 N. West Street

Alexandria, VA 22314

Phone: 800-372-1924

Email: news-fra@fra.org

http://www.fra.org

Purpose: To recognize outstanding student essayists.

Eligibility: Applicants must be in grades 7 through 12 and must be sponsored by a Fleet Reserve Association (FRA) branch or Ladies Auxiliary unit. They must submit an essay on a sponsor-determined topic. Selection is based on the overall strength of the essay.

Amount: $2,500-$5,000.

Number of Awards: Varies.

Deadline: December 1.

How to Apply: Entry instructions are available online. An essay and cover sheet are required.

Americorps National Civilian Community Corps

AmeriCorps

1201 New York Avenue NW

Washington, DC 20525

Phone: 202-606-5000

Fax: 202-606-3472

Email: questions@americorps.org

http://www.americorps.gov

Purpose: To strengthen communities and develop leaders through community service.

Eligibility: Applicants must be U.S. citizens who are between 18 and 24 years of age. Recipients must live on one of five AmeriCorps campuses in Denver, Colorado; Sacramento, California; Baltimore, Maryland; Vinton, Iowa or Vicksburg, Mississippi. Applicants must commit to 10 months of service on projects in areas such as education, public safety, the environment and other unmet needs. The projects are located within the region of one of the four campuses.

Amount: $5,775.

Number of Awards: Varies.

Deadline: Varies.

How to Apply: Applications are available online.

Americorps Vista

AmeriCorps

1201 New York Avenue NW

Washington, DC 20525

Phone: 202-606-5000

Fax: 202-606-3472

Email: questions@americorps.org

http://www.americorps.gov

Purpose: To provide education assistance in exchange for community service.

Eligibility: Applicants must be United States citizens who are at least 17 years of age. They must be available to serve full-time for one year at a nonprofit organization or local government agency with an objective that may

include to fight illiteracy, improve health services, create businesses or strengthen community groups.
Amount: Varies.
Number of Awards: Varies.
Deadline: Varies.
How to Apply: Applications are available online.

Anthem Essay Contest

Ayn Rand Institute Anthem Essay Contest
Department W
P.O. Box 57044
Irvine, CA 92619-7044
Phone: 949-222-6550
Fax: 949-222-6558
Email: essay@aynrand.org
http://www.aynrand.org
Purpose: To honor high school students who distinguish themselves in their understanding of Ayn Rand's novel *Anthem.*
Eligibility: Applicants must be eighth, ninth or tenth grade students who submit a 600-1,200-word essay that will be judged on both style and content, with an emphasis on writing that is clear, articulate and logically organized. Winning essays must demonstrate an outstanding grasp of the philosophic meaning of *Anthem.*
Amount: Up to $2,000.
Number of Awards: 236.
Deadline: May 1.
How to Apply: Application request information is available online.

Apartment List Scholarship

Apartment List
500 3rd Street, Suite 555
San Francisco, CA 94107
http://www.apartmentlist.com/scholarship
Purpose: To support students who exemplify one or more of Apartment List's core values.

Eligibility: Applicants must be at least 18 years of age, a U.S. resident and a high school senior or currently enrolled undergraduate or graduate level student. Students must provide in a short essay proof of representing one of Apartment List's core values of forever learning, driven by data, making an impact, bold while pragmatic, endlessly helpful and succeeding together. A second short essay describing "what is most important to you in choosing a place to call 'home'" is required. **Amount:** $2,500.
Number of Awards: 1.
Deadline: March 1; September 1.
How to Apply: Applications are available online.

Art Awards

Scholastic Art and Writing Awards
557 Broadway
New York, NY 10012
Phone: 212-343-6100
Fax: 212-389-3939
Email: info@artandwriting.org
http://www.artandwriting.org/scholarships/
Purpose: To reward America's best student artists.
Eligibility: Applicants must be in grades 7 through 12 in American or Canadian schools and must submit artwork in one of the following categories: art portfolio, animation, ceramics and glass, computer art, design, digital imagery, drawing, mixed media, painting, photography, photography portfolio, printmaking, sculpture or video and film. There are regional and national levels.
Amount: Varies.
Number of Awards: Varies.
Deadline: Varies.
How to Apply: Applications are available online. The deadlines vary by state but start in December. There is an online form to find out the deadline for your state.

Atlas Shrugged Essay Contest

Ayn Rand Institute Atlas Shrugged
Essay Contest
Department W
P.O. Box 57044
Irvine, CA 92619-7044
Phone: 949-222-6550
Fax: 949-222-6558
Email: essays@aynrand.org
https://www.aynrand.org/contests
Purpose: To honor students who
distinguish themselves in their
understanding of Ayn Rand's novel
Atlas Shrugged.
Eligibility: Applicants must be high
school seniors, college undergraduates
or graduate students who submit an
800-1,600-word essay which will be
judged on both style and content with
an emphasis on writing that is clear,
articulate and logically organized.
Winning essays must demonstrate an
outstanding grasp of the philosophic
meaning of *Atlas Shrugged.*
Amount: Up to $10,000.
Number of Awards: 236.
Deadline: May 15.
How to Apply: Application request
information is available online.

AU Student Essay Contest

Americans United for Separation of
Church and State
Attn.: Essay Contest Submission
1901 L Street NW
Suite 400
Washington, DC 20036
Phone: 202-466-3234 x427
Email: campus@au.org
https://au.org/
Purpose: To emphasize the importance
of the separation of church and state.
Eligibility: Applicants must be current
high school juniors or seniors in the
U.S. Students must submit an essay
discussing potential violations of church-
state separations in public schools.
Amount: $1,500.

Number of Awards: 3.
Deadline: April 15.
How to Apply: Applications are
available online.

AXA Achievement Scholarships

c/o Scholarship America
One Scholarship Way
St. Peter, MN 56082
Phone: 800-537-4180
Email: axaachievement@
scholarshipamerica.org
https://us.axa.com/axa-foundation/
about.html
Purpose: To provide financial
assistance to ambitious students.
Eligibility: Applicants must be U.S.
citizens or legal residents who are
current high school seniors and are
planning to enroll full-time in an
accredited college or university in
the fall following their graduation.
They must show ambition and drive
evidenced by outstanding achievement
in school, community or workplace
activities. A recommendation from an
unrelated adult who can vouch for the
student's achievement is required.
Amount: $2,500.
Number of Awards: Up to 12.
Deadline: December 15.
How to Apply: Applications are
available online.

BankMobile Financial Literacy Scholarship

BankMobile
401 Park Avenue South
New York, NY 10016
Phone: 917-941-4704
Email: scholarship@bankmobile.com
http://www.bankmobile.com
Purpose: To support student financial
literacy.
Eligibility: Applicants must be
undergraduate or graduate level
students, U.S. citizens and have a

minimum 3.0 GPA. Students must submit an essay explaining the importance of financial literacy in both their lives and their career. Special consideration is given to applicants who are actively promoting financial literacy within their community.

Amount: $1,500.

Number of Awards: 1.

Deadline: July 19.

How to Apply: Applications are available online and must include an official transcript (high school or college) and the essay.

Bob Bennett Memorial Scholarship

Unity One Credit Union
6701 Burlington Boulevard
Fort Worth, TX 76131
Phone: 817-306- 3100
Fax: 817-306-3101
http://info.unityone.org/blog/unity-one-cu-informs-apply-for-the-bob-bennett-scholarship

Purpose: To support students pursuing a higher education.

Eligibility: Applicants must be either graduating high school seniors or current college students. Students must write an essay as part of their application.

Amount: $250-$1,000.

Number of Awards: 3.

Deadline: April 28.

How to Apply: Applications are available online.

Bruce Lee Foundation Scholarship Program

Bruce Lee Foundation
11693 San Vicente Boulevard
Suite 918
Los Angeles , CA 90049
Email: info@bruceleefoundation.org
http://www.bruceleefoundation.com

Purpose: To support students attending or planning to attend college and

who also exude Bruce Lee's love for education.

Eligibility: Applicants must be at least 16 years of age and be attending or planning to attend a two-year or four-year college or university or trade/vocational school within the United States. Applicants must also hold a passion for education and value the characteristics exemplified by Bruce Lee. Students may be interviewed by phone if chosen as final contenders. Selection is based upon the overall strength of the application.

Amount: $2,500-$10,000.

Number of Awards: 5.

Deadline: June 9.

How to Apply: Applications are available online. An application form and two letters of recommendation are required.

Bruce Lee Scholarship

U.S. Pan Asian American Chamber of Commerce
1329 18th Street NW
Washington, DC 20036
Phone: 800-696-7818
Fax: 202-296-5225
Email: info@uspaacc.com
http://uspaacc.com/

Purpose: To support the higher education goals of students of all ethnic backgrounds.

Eligibility: Applicants must be U.S. citizens or permanent residents and be high school seniors who will pursue post-secondary educations at an accredited institution in the U.S. Students do not need to be Asian Americans. Selection is based on character, the ability to persevere over adversity, academic excellence with at least a 3.3 GPA, community service involvement and financial need. Applicants must be able to attend the Excellence Awards and Scholarships Dinner during the CelebrAsian Annual Conference (in May).

Amount: Varies.
Number of Awards: Varies.
Deadline: March 17.
How to Apply: Applications are available online.

Burger King Scholars Program

5505 Blue Lagoon Drive
Miami, FL 33126
Phone: 305-378-3000
Email: bdorado@whopper.com
http://www.bkmclamorefoundation.org
Purpose: To provide financial assistance for high school seniors who have part-time jobs.
Eligibility: Applicants may apply from public, private, vocational, technical, parochial and alternative high schools in the United States, Canada and Puerto Rico and must be U.S. or Canadian residents. Students must also have a minimum 2.5 GPA, work part-time an average of 15 hours per week unless there are extenuating circumstances, participate in community service or other activities, demonstrate financial need and plan to enroll in an accredited two- or four-year college, university or vocational/technical school by the fall term of the graduating year. Applicants do NOT need to work at Burger King, but Burger King employees are eligible.
Amount: $1,000-$50,000.
Number of Awards: Varies.
Deadline: December 15.
How to Apply: Applications are available online and may only be completed online.

C.I.P. Scholarship

College Is Power
1025 Alameda de las Pulgas
No. 215
Belmont, CA 94002
http://www.collegeispower.com/scholarship.cfm
Purpose: To assist adult students age 18 and over with college expenses.

Eligibility: Applicants must be adult students currently attending or planning to attend a two-year or four-year college or university within the next 12 months. Students must be 18 years or older and U.S. citizens or permanent residents. The award may be used for full- or part-time study at either on-campus or online schools.
Amount: $1,000.
Number of Awards: Varies.
Deadline: December 31.
How to Apply: Applications are available online.

Carson Scholars

305 W Chesapeake Avenue
Suite 310
Towson, MD 21204
Phone: 877-773-7236
Fax: 410-828-1007
Email: katie@carsonscholars.org
http://carsonscholars.org/scholarships/
Purpose: To recognize students who demonstrate academic excellence and commitment to the community.
Eligibility: Applicants must be nominated by their school. They must be in grades 4 through 11 and have a GPA of 3.75 or higher in English, reading, language arts, math, science, social studies and foreign language. They must have participated in some form of voluntary community service beyond what is required by their school. Scholarship recipients must attend a four-year college or university upon graduation to receive funds.
Amount: $1,000.
Number of Awards: Varies.
Deadline: January 8.
How to Apply: Applications are available from the schools of those nominated. Only one student per school may be nominated.

Christophers Video Contest for College Students

Christophers
5 Hanover Square
22nd Floor
New York, NY 10004
Phone: 212-759-4050
Fax: 212-838-5073
Email: youth@christophers.org
http://www.christophers.org
Purpose: To support college students who believe in The Christophers' mission that any one person can make a difference.
Eligibility: Applicants must be current undergraduate or graduate level college students and U.S. citizens. Selection is based on the video submitted and how well it depicts the theme of "One Person Can Make a Difference."
Amount: $500-$2,000.
Number of Awards: 3.
Deadline: December 15.
How to Apply: Applications are available online. Students must also submit a video of five minutes or less communicating the theme.

CKSF Scholarships

Common Knowledge Scholarship Foundation
P.O. Box 290361
Davie, FL 33329-0361
Phone: 954-262-8553
Email: info@cksf.org
http://www.cksf.org
Purpose: To support high school and college students.
Eligibility: Applicants must register online with CKSF and complete quizzes on various topics. Students may be U.S. high school students in grades 9 to 12 or college students.
Amount: $250-$2,500.
Number of Awards: Varies.
Deadline: Monthly.

How to Apply: Applications are available online. Online registration is required.

Coca-Cola All-State Community College Academic Team

Coca-Cola Scholars Foundation
P.O. Box 442
Atlanta, GA 30301
Phone: 800-306-2653
Email: Scholars@coca-cola.com
http://www.coca-colascholarsfoundation.org/apply/
Purpose: To assist community college students with college expenses.
Eligibility: Applicants must be enrolled in community college, have a minimum GPA of 3.5 on a four-point scale and be on track to earn an associate's or bachelor's degree. Students attending community college in the U.S. do NOT need to be members of Phi Theta Kappa. Fifty students will win a $1,500 scholarship, fifty students will win a $1,250 scholarship and fifty students will win a $1,000 scholarship.
Amount: $1,000-$1,500.
Number of Awards: 200.
Deadline: December 6.
How to Apply: Applications are available online. Nomination from the designated nominator at your school is required. A list of nominators is available at http://www.ptk.org.

Coca-Cola Scholars Program

Coca-Cola Scholars Foundation
P.O. Box 442
Atlanta, GA 30301
Phone: 800-306-2653
Email: Scholars@coca-cola.com
http://www.coca-colascholarsfoundation.org/apply/
Purpose: Begun in 1986 to celebrate the Coca-Cola Centennial, the program is designed to contribute to the nation's future and to assist a wide range of students.

Eligibility: Applicants must be high school seniors in the U.S., be U.S. citizens, nationals or permanent residents and must use the awards at an accredited U.S. college or university. Selection is based on the transcript, school profile, school and non-school related clubs and organizations, honors and awards and volunteer service.
Amount: $20,000.
Number of Awards: 150.
Scholarship may be renewable.
Deadline: October 31.
How to Apply: Applications are available online.

CollegeNET Scholarships

CollegeNET Scholarship Review Committee
805 SW Broadway
Suite 1600
Portland, OR 97205
Phone: 503-973-5200
Fax: 503-973-5252
Email: scholarship@collegenet.com
http://www.collegenet.com
Purpose: To assist college applicants.
Eligibility: Applicants must sign up at the website and visit and participate in forums. Recipients are determined by votes on the website.
Amount: Varies.
Number of Awards: Varies.
Deadline: Weekly.
How to Apply: Applications are available online.

Coolidge Scholarship

Calvin Coolidge Memorial Foundation Inc.
P.O. Box 97
Plymouth, VT 05056
Phone: 802-672-3389
Email: coolidgescholars@ coolidgefoundation.org
https://coolidgescholars.org/
Purpose: To reward high school juniors who have achieved academic excellence

and have an interest in public policy.
Eligibility: Applicants must be U.S. citizens planning on enrolling full-time in an accredited U.S. college or university. Students must apply during their junior year in high school. Selection is based on academic excellence, interest in public policy and appreciation for Coolidge values and demonstrated humility and leadership.
Amount: Full ride.
Number of Awards: 2.
Deadline: January 24.
How to Apply: Applications are available online through the website and include an essay, a transcript, a resume and two letters of recommendation.

Copyright Awareness Scholarship

Music Publishers Association of the United States
243 5th Avenue
Suite 236
New York, NY 10016
Email: scholarship@mpa.org
http://www.mpa.org
Purpose: To support students interested in educating their peers via video about the laws surrounding intellectual property and copyright.
Eligibility: Applicants must be legal residents of the U.S. and be currently enrolled at a college, university or trade school in the United States. They must be between 13 and 25 years of age. A video submission that accurately illustrates the applicant's viewpoint of the importance of Intellectual Property and Copyright Law is required. Selection is based on the overall quality of the video submission.
Amount: $2,000-$5,000.
Number of Awards: 3.
Deadline: May 21.
How to Apply: Application with video submission must be submitted online.

Create Real Impact Contest

Impact Teen Drivers
Attn.: Create Real Impact Contest
P.O. Box 161209
Sacramento, CA 95816
Phone: 916-733-7432
Email: info@impactteendrivers.org
http://www.createrealimpact.com
Purpose: To raise awareness of the dangers of distracted driving and poor decision making.
Eligibility: Applicants must be legal U.S. residents who are between the ages of 14 and 22. They must be enrolled full-time at an accredited secondary or post-secondary school. They must submit an original, videotaped creative project that offers a solution to the problem of distracted driving. Selection is based on project concept, message effectiveness and creativity.
Amount: $500 and $1,500.
Number of Awards: 13.
Deadline: March 17.
How to Apply: Contest entry instructions are available online. A videotaped creative project is required.

Create-a-Greeting-Card Scholarship

Gallery Collection
Prudent Publishing
65 Challenger Road
P.O. Box 150
Ridgefield Park, NJ 07660
Phone: 800-950-7064
Fax: 800-772-1144
Email: service@gallerycollection.com
https://www.gallerycollection.com/greeting-cards-scholarship.htm
Purpose: To reward high school, college students and members of the United States armed forces who enter a contest to create a Christmas card, holiday card, birthday card or all-occasion greeting card.
Eligibility: Applicants must be U.S. citizens or legal residents who are at least 14 years old. The submission must include original artwork or photographs. Those members of the United States armed forces must not be older than 34. Selection is based on the overall quality of the submission including creativity, uniqueness and suitability.
Amount: $1,000-$10,000.
Number of Awards: 2.
Deadline: March 2.
How to Apply: Applications and submissions may be made online or mailed directly to the scholarship administrator at the Gallery Collection. Entry form and greeting card submission are required. Online submissions are preferred.

Davidson Fellows Scholarships

Davidson Institute for Talent Development
9665 Gateway Drive
Suite B
Reno, NV 89521
Phone: 775-852-3483
Email: DavidsonFellows@davidsongifted.org
http://www.davidsongifted.org/
Purpose: To reward young people for their works in mathematics, science, technology, music, literature, philosophy or "outside the box."
Eligibility: Applicants must be under the age of 18 and be able to attend the awards reception in Washington, DC. In addition to the monetary award, the institute will pay for travel and lodging expenses. Three nominator forms, three copies of a 15-minute DVD and additional materials are required.
Amount: $10,000-$50,000.
Number of Awards: Varies.
Deadline: February 8.
How to Apply: Applications are available online.

Davis-Putter Scholarship Fund

P.O. Box 7307
New York, NY 10116

Email: information@davisputter.org
http://www.davisputter.org
Purpose: To assist students who are both academically capable and who aid the progressive movement for peace and justice both on campus and in their communities.
Eligibility: Applicants must be undergraduate or graduate students who participate in the progressive movement, acting in the interests of issues such as expansion of civil rights and international solidarity, among others. Applicants must also have demonstrated financial need as well as a solid academic record.
Amount: Up to $10,000.
Number of Awards: Varies.
Deadline: April 1.
How to Apply: Applications are available online.

Delete Cyberbullying Scholarship Award

Delete Cyberbullying
2261 Market Street #291
San Francisco, CA 94114
Email: help@deletecyberbullying.org
http://www.deletecyberbullying.org
Purpose: To get students committed to the cause of deleting cyberbullying.
Eligibility: Applicants must be a U.S. citizen or permanent resident and attending or planning to attend an accredited U.S. college or university for undergraduate or graduate studies. Applicants must also be a high school, college or graduate student or a student planning to enter college.
Amount: $1,000.
Number of Awards: 1.
Deadline: June 30.
How to Apply: Applications are available online. An application form and an essay are required.

Dell Scholars Program

Michael and Susan Dell Foundation
P.O. Box 163867
Austin, TX 78716
Phone: 512-329-0799
Fax: 512-347-1744
Email: apply@dellscholars.org
http://www.dellscholars.org
Purpose: To support underprivileged high school seniors.
Eligibility: Students must be participants in an approved college readiness program, and they must have at least a 2.4 GPA. Applicants must be pursuing a bachelor's degree in the fall directly after graduation. Students must also be U.S. citizens or permanent residents and demonstrate financial need. Selection is based on "individual determination to succeed," future goals, hardships that have been overcome, self motivation and financial need.
Amount: Varies.
Number of Awards: Varies. Scholarship may be renewable.
Deadline: January 15.
How to Apply: Applications are available online. An online application is required.

Digital Privacy Scholarship

Digital Responsibility
3561 Homestead Road #113
Santa Clara, CA 95051-5161
Email: scholarship@digitalresponsibility.org
http://www.digitalresponsibility.org
Purpose: To help students understand why it's important to be cautious about what they post on the Internet.
Eligibility: Applicants must be a high school freshman, sophomore, junior or senior or a current or entering college or graduate school student of any level. Home schooled students are also eligible. There is no age limit. Students must also be a U.S. citizen or legal resident.

Amount: $1,000.
Number of Awards: 1.
Deadline: June 30.
How to Apply: Applications are available online.

DirectTextbook.com Photo Essay Contest

DirectTextbook.com
1525 Chemeketa Street NE
Salem, OR 97301
Phone: 503-779-4056
Email: service@directtextbook.com
http://www.directtextbook.com/scholarship.php
Purpose: To assist students who submit photos.
Eligibility: Applicants must be U.S. citizens who are current two- or four-year college students and who have a minimum 2.0 GPA. Students must submit a photo based on the theme given.
Amount: $250-$1,000.
Number of Awards: 3.
Deadline: January 16.
How to Apply: Applications are available online.

DirectTextbook.com Scholarship Essay Contest

DirectTextbook.com
1525 Chemeketa Street NE
Salem, OR 97301
Phone: 503-779-4056
Email: service@directtextbook.com
http://www.directtextbook.com/scholarship.php
Purpose: To support students who write an essay.
Eligibility: Applicants must be U.S. citizens who will attend a two-year college, four-year college or university or post-graduate school in the fall. Students must have a grade point average of 2.0 or higher. Applicants must provide completed application and essay.

Amount: $1,000-$5,000.
Number of Awards: 3.
Deadline: July 25.
How to Apply: Applications are available online.

Distinguished Young Women Scholarship Program

Distinguished Young Women
751 Government Street
Mobile, AL 36602
Phone: 251-438-3621
Fax: 251-431-0063
Email: lynne@ajm.org
http://distinguishedyw.org/scholarships/
Purpose: To provide scholarship opportunities and encourage personal development for high school girls through a competitive pageant stressing academics and talent as well as self-expression and fitness.
Eligibility: Teen girls are selected from state competitions to participate in a national pageant. Contestants are judged on a combination of scholastics, personal interview, talent, fitness and self-expression. Applicants should be a high school student at least in their sophomore year. Students must be U.S. citizens, have never been married and have never been pregnant.
Amount: Varies.
Number of Awards: Varies.
Deadline: Varies.
How to Apply: Applications are available online.

Don't Text and Drive Scholarship

Digital Responsibility
3561 Homestead Road #113
Santa Clara, CA 95051-5161
Email: scholarship@digitalresponsibility.org
http://www.digitalresponsibility.org
Purpose: To help students understand the risks of texting while driving.

Eligibility: Applicants must be a high school freshman, sophomore, junior or senior or a current or entering college or graduate school student of any level. Home schooled students are also eligible. There is no age limit. Students must also be a U.S. citizen or legal resident.

Amount: $1,000.

Number of Awards: 1.

Deadline: September 30.

How to Apply: Applications are available online.

DoSomething.org Seasonal Scholarships

Do Something (Scholarships)
19 West 21st Street, Floor 8
New York, NY 10010
Phone: 212-254-2390
Email: scholarships@dosomething.org
https://www.dosomething.org/us/about/easy-scholarships

Purpose: To assist students who participate in a social issue campaign.

Eligibility: Applicants must be age 25 or younger and be U.S. or Canadian citizens. There is a new scholarship each quarter. Selection is based on a random drawing of all students who participate in the campaign.

Amount: Varies.

Number of Awards: Varies.

Deadline: Varies.

How to Apply: Applications are available online.

Dr. Alma S. Adams Scholarship

Truth Initiative
900 G Street, NW
Fourth Floor
Washington, DC 20001
Phone: 202-454-5555
Email: adamsscholarship@truthinititative.org
http://truthinitiative.org/Adams-Scholarship

Purpose: To support students who have a passion to help reduce the use of tobacco products in priority underserved populations.

Eligibility: Applicants must be U.S. citizens or legal residents. Students should be pursuing a degree in public health, communications, social work, education, liberal arts or related field and have a minimum GPA of 2.0. Applicants must provide proof of community service activities such as (but not limited to) activism, outreach or peer counseling in tobacco prevention or control. Financial need is considered.

Amount: $5,000.

Number of Awards: 2.

Deadline: April 30.

How to Apply: Applications are available online and must include a SAR report.

E-waste Scholarship

Digital Responsibility
3561 Homestead Road #113
Santa Clara, CA 95051-5161
Email: scholarship@digitalresponsibility.org
http://www.digitalresponsibility.org

Purpose: To help students understand the impact of e-waste and what can be done to reduce e-waste.

Eligibility: Applicants must be a high school, college, graduate or home schooled students. There is no age limit. Students must also be a U.S. citizen or legal resident. A 140-character message about e-waste is required to apply. The top 10 applications will be selected as finalists; finalists will be asked to write a full length 500- to 1,000-word essay about e-waste. Only online applications are accepted.

Amount: $1,000.

Number of Awards: 1.

Deadline: April 30.

How to Apply: Applications are available online.

eCampus Tours Scholarship Giveaway

Edsouth
eCampusTours
P.O. Box 36014
Knoxville, TN 37930
Phone: 865-342-0670
Email: info@ecampustours.com
http://www.ecampustours.com
Purpose: To assist students in paying for college.
Eligibility: Eligible students include U.S. citizens, U.S. nationals and permanent residents or students enrolled in a U.S. institution of higher education. Winners must be enrolled in an eligible institution of higher education, as stipulated in the eligibility requirements, within one year of winning the award. Scholarship awards will be paid directly to the college.
Amount: $1,000.
Number of Awards: 2.
Deadline: March 31.
How to Apply: Applications are available online or by mail. Registration with eCampusTours is required.

Educational Advancement Foundation Merit Scholarship

Alpha Kappa Alpha Educational Advancement Foundation Inc.
5656 S. Stony Island Avenue
Chicago, IL 60637
Phone: 800-653-6528
Fax: 773-947-0277
Email: akaeaf@akaeaf.net
https://akaeaf.org/scholarships
Purpose: To support academically talented students.
Eligibility: Applicants must be full-time college students at the sophomore level or higher, including graduate students, at an accredited school. They must have a GPA of at least 3.0 and demonstrate community involvement and service. The program is open to students

without regard to sex, race, creed, color, ethnicity, religion, sexual orientation or disability. Students do NOT need to be members of Alpha Kappa Alpha. The application deadline is April 15 for undergraduates and August 15 for graduates.
Amount: Varies.
Number of Awards: Varies.
Deadline: April 15 (undergraduates) and August 15 (graduates).
How to Apply: Applications are available online. An application form, personal statement and three letters of recommendation are required.

Family Travel Forum Teen Travel Writing Scholarship

Family Travel Forum
135 West 20th Street
5th Floor
New York, NY 10011
Phone: 212-595-6074
Fax: 212-665-6136
Email: editorial@travelbigo.com
http://scholarship.familytravelforum.com
Purpose: To aid college-bound students who have written the best travel essays.
Eligibility: Applicants must be members of the MyFamilyTravels.com online community and be between the ages of 13 and 18. They must be in grades 8 through 12 and must be attending a U.S. or Canadian high school, U.S. or Canadian junior high school, U.S. home school or an American school located outside of the U.S. They must submit an essay about a significant travel experience that occurred within the past five years and that happened when the applicant was between the ages of 12 and 18. Selection is based on originality, quality of storytelling and grammar.
Amount: $1,000.
Number of Awards: 3.
Deadline: July 14.
How to Apply: Application

instructions are available online. An essay submission form and essay are required.

Foreclosure.com Scholarship Program

Foreclosure.com
1095 Broken Sound Parkway, NW
Suite 200
Boca Raton, FL 33487
Phone: 561-988-9669 x 7387
Email: scholarship@foreclosure.com
http://www.foreclosure.com/scholarship/

Purpose: To support current undergraduate college students who are interested in addressing critical issues facing the nation, namely issues involving real estate/housing.

Eligibility: Applicants must be U.S. citizens 13 years of age or older who are currently enrolled as undergraduate college students. They must write an essay between 800 and 2,000 words providing creative solutions to a given topic involving critical issues facing the nation centered around real estate/housing. Selection is based upon the overall strength of the essay and application.

Amount: $1,000-$5,000.

Number of Awards: 5.

Deadline: December 15.

How to Apply: Applications are available online. An application form and essay are required.

Fostering the Entrepreneurial Spirit: A Contest for High School Students

Ed Snider Center for Enterprise and Markets
4568 Van Munching Hall
College Park, MD 20742
Phone: 301-405-7036
Email: info@enterpriselit.org
http://www.enterpriselit.org

Purpose: To promote the entrepreneurial spirit in high school students through works of literature.

Eligibility: Applicants must be in grades 9-12. Students will work in teams of two to four and choose a work of literature that emphasizes the struggles and achievements of a person seeking to become an entrepreneur. The book will then be compared to real-life entrepreneurs. Teams will submit an essay outlining the main character and his/her contributions to the theme of the book including works cited and also a video that visually demonstrates what was learned during the project.

Amount: $200-$1,500.

Number of Awards: 8.

Deadline: May 2.

How to Apply: Applications are available online and include an essay and video.

Fountainhead Essay Contest

Ayn Rand Institute Fountainhead Essay Contest
Department W
P.O. Box 57044
Irvine, CA 92619-7044
Phone: 949-222-6550
Fax: 949-222-6558
Email: essays@aynrand.org
https://www.aynrand.org/contests

Purpose: To honor high school students who distinguish themselves in their understanding of Ayn Rand's novel *The Fountainhead*.

Eligibility: Applicants must be high school juniors or seniors who submit a 800-1,600 word essay which will be judged on both style and content with an emphasis on writing that is clear, articulate and logically organized. Winning essays must demonstrate an outstanding grasp of the philosophic and psychological meaning of *The Fountainhead*.

Amount: $50-$10,000.

Number of Awards: 236.

Deadline: May 15.

How to Apply: Application request information is available online.

Frame My Future Scholarship Contest

Church Hill Classics
594 Pepper Street
Monroe, CT 06468
Phone: 800-477-9005
Fax: 203-268-2468
Email: info@diplomaframe.com
http://www.diplomaframe.com
Purpose: To help success-driven students attain their higher education goals.
Eligibility: Applicants must be high school seniors or otherwise eligible for graduation in the school year of application or current college students. They must plan to enroll in college full-time the following academic year. Applicants must be residents of the United States, including APO/FPO addresses but excluding Puerto Rico. Employees of Church Hill Classics and affiliated companies, their family members and individuals living in the same household are not eligible. A photograph, collage, poem, drawing, painting, graphic design piece, short typed explanation or other creative entry is required to demonstrate what the applicants want to achieve in their personal and professional life after college.
Amount: $1,000.
Number of Awards: 5.
Deadline: March 1.
How to Apply: Applications must be submitted online. An entry form and original piece of artwork are required.

Free Community College Story Competition

Heads Up America
727 15th Street NW
3rd Floor
Washington, DC 20005
Phone: 202-507-9597
Email: collegepromise@civicnation.org
http://headsupamerica.us/i-will/
Purpose: To assist students pursuing community college education.
Eligibility: Applicant must be U.S. residents at least 16 years of age. Students must create a one minute video to be posted on social media that describes their aspirations and potential accomplishments with free community college.
Amount: $2,000.
Number of Awards: 1.
Deadline: October 15.
How to Apply: Applications are available online.

Freedom of Speech PSA Contest

National Association of Broadcasters
1771 N Street NW
Washington, DC 20036
Phone: 202-429-5428
Email: nab@nab.org
http://www.nab.org
Purpose: To reward part-time or full-time undergraduate or graduate students who can effectively illustrate what freedom of speech means to them and what part it plays in the world today in a 30-second public service announcement.
Eligibility: Applicants must be part-time or full-time graduate or undergraduate students currently attending a college, university or technical/community college. They must create a 30-second public service announcement while enrolled answering the question, "What does freedom of speech mean to me?" Announcements may be created for television or radio. Selection is based upon quality of submission.
Amount: $1,000-$3,000.
Number of Awards: 4.
Deadline: April 30.
How to Apply: Applications are available online.

Fulbright Grants

U.S. Department of State
Office of Academic Exchange
Programs, Bureau of Educational and
Cultural Affairs
U.S. Department of State, SA-44
301 4th Street SW, Room 234
Washington, DC 20547
Phone: 202-632-3238
Fax: 202-401-5914
Email: fulbright@state.gov
https://us.fulbrightonline.org/
Purpose: To increase the understanding
between the people of the United States
and the people of other countries.
Eligibility: Applicants must be
graduating college seniors, graduate
students, young professionals and
artists. Funds are generally used to
support students in university teaching,
advanced research, graduate study or
teaching in elementary and secondary
schools.
Amount: Varies.
Number of Awards: Varies.
Deadline: October 15.
How to Apply: Applications are
available online.

GE-Reagan Foundation Scholarship Program

Ronald Reagan Presidential Foundation
40 Presidential Drive, Suite 200
Simi Valley, CA 93065
Phone: 507-931-1682
Email: ge-reagan@scholarshipamerica.
org
http://www.scholarshipamerica.org/
ge-reagan
Purpose: To reward students who
demonstrate leadership, drive, integrity
and citizenship.
Eligibility: Applicants must be high
school seniors and pursue a bachelor's
degree at an accredited U.S. college or
university the following fall. Students
must demonstrate strong academic
performance (3.0 or greater GPA or

equivalent), demonstrate financial need
and be a U.S. citizen. Funds may be
used for student tuition and room and
board.
Amount: $10,000.
Number of Awards: Up to 20.
Scholarship may be renewable.
Deadline: January 9.
How to Apply: Applications are
available online. The competition will
close earlier than the deadline once
25,000 applications are received.

Gen and Kelly Tanabe Student Scholarship

2713 Newlands Avenue
Belmont, CA 94002
Phone: 650-618-2221
Email: scholarships@gkscholarship.com
http://www.genkellyscholarship.com
Purpose: To assist high school, college
and graduate school students with
educational expenses.
Eligibility: Applicants must be 9th-12th
grade high school students, college
students or graduate school students
who are legal U.S. residents. Students
may study any major and attend any
college in the U.S.
Amount: $1,000.
Deadline: December 31.
How to Apply: Applications are
available online.

George Montgomery/NRA Youth Wildlife Art Contest

National Rifle Association
11250 Waples Mill Road
Fairfax, VA 22030
Phone: 800-672-3888
Email: grantprogram@nrahq.org
https://awards.nra.org/awards/
Purpose: To support young artists and
encourage awareness of local game
birds and animals.
Eligibility: Applicants must be in
grades 1 through 12 and submit an
original artwork depicting any North

American game bird or animal that may be legally hunted or trapped. NRA membership is not required. Art is divided into categories based on grade level and is judged on effort, creativity, anatomical accuracy and composition.
Amount: Up to $1,000.
Number of Awards: Varies.
Deadline: November 3.
How to Apply: Application information is available online. A statement of authenticity signed by a parent, guardian or teacher must be submitted along with the artwork.

George S. and Stella M. Knight Essay Contest

National Society, Sons of the American Revolution
1000 South Fourth Street
Louisville, KY 40203
Phone: 502-589-1776
Fax: 502-589-1671
Email: sdelong1@san.rr.com
http://www.sar.org
Purpose: To reward students who have written outstanding essays on the American Revolution, the U.S. Constitution or the Declaration of Independence.
Eligibility: Applicants must be U.S. citizens or legal residents. Students must be high school sophomores, juniors or seniors. Applicants must submit an 800- to 1,200-word essay on some topic that is related to the Declaration of Independence, the American Revolution or the U.S. Constitution. Selection is based on the overall strength of the essay.
Amount: $1,000-$5,000.
Number of Awards: 3.
Deadline: December 31.
How to Apply: Applications are available online.

Horatio Alger Association Scholarship Program

Horatio Alger Association
Attn.: Scholarship Department
99 Canal Center Plaza
Suite 320
Alexandria, VA 22314
Phone: 703-684-9444
Fax: 703-548-3822
Email: association@horatioalger.org
https://scholars.horatioalger.org/
Purpose: To assist students who are committed to pursuing a bachelor's degree and have demonstrated integrity, financial need, academic achievement and community involvement.
Eligibility: Applicants must enter college the fall following their high school graduation, have at least a 2.0 GPA, be in need of financial aid ($55,000 or less adjusted gross income per family is preferred) and be involved in extracurricular and community activities. Students applying from Louisiana, Montana and Idaho have additional state specific requirements.
Amount: $25,000.
Number of Awards: 106.
Deadline: October 25.
How to Apply: Applications are available online.

IAPMO Essay Scholarship Contest

International Association of Plumbing and Mechanical Officials (IAPMO)
4755 E. Philadelphia Street
Ontario, CA 91761
Phone: 909-472-4100
Fax: 909-472-4222
Email: gaby.davis@iapmo.org
http://www.iapmo.org/Pages/EssayContest.aspx
Purpose: To share the "importance the plumbing and mechanical industry plays in our everyday lives."
Eligibility: Applicants must be current high school seniors or enrolled or

accepted as full-time students in an accredited technical school, community college, trade school, four-year accredited college or university or an apprentice program.
Amount: $500-$1,000.
Number of Awards: 3.
Deadline: May 1.
How to Apply: Applications are available online. An essay of 800 to 1,600 words on the topic provided is required.

Jack Kent Cooke Foundation College Scholarship Program

Jack Kent Cooke Foundation
44325 Woodridge Parkway
Lansdowne, VA 20176
Phone: 800-941-3300
Fax: 703-723-8030
Email: scholarships@jkcf.org
http://www.jkcf.org
Purpose: To assist high school seniors with financial need.
Eligibility: Applicants must plan to graduate from a U.S. high school in the spring and plan to enroll in an accredited four-year college beginning in the fall following application. Students must have a minimum 3.5 GPA and have standardized test scores in the top 15 percent: SAT combined critical reading and math score of 1200 or above and/or ACT composite score of 26 or above. Applicants must also demonstrate significant unmet financial need. Family incomes up to $95,000 are considered. However, the majority of recipients will be eligible to receive a Pell grant.
Amount: Up to $40,000 per year for four years.
Number of Awards: Up to 40. Scholarship may be renewable.
Deadline: Late November.
How to Apply: Applications are available online.

Jeannette Rankin Women's Scholarship Fund

Jeannette Rankin Foundation
1 Huntington Road
Suite 701
Athens, GA 30606
Phone: 706-208-1211
Email: info@rankinfoundation.org
http://www.rankinfoundation.org
Purpose: To support the education of low-income women 35 years or older.
Eligibility: Applicants must be women 35 years of age or older, plan to obtain an undergraduate or vocational education and meet maximum household income guidelines.
Amount: Varies.
Number of Awards: Varies. Scholarship may be renewable.
Deadline: March 18.
How to Apply: Applications are available online or by sending a self-addressed and stamped envelope to the foundation.

John F. Kennedy Profile in Courage Essay Contest

John F. Kennedy Library Foundation
Columbia Point
Boston, MA 02125
Phone: 617-514-1649
Email: profiles@nara.gov
http://www.jfklibrary.org/
Purpose: To encourage students to research and write about politics and John F. Kennedy.
Eligibility: Applicants must be in grades 9 through 12 in public or private schools or be home-schooled and write an essay about the political courage of a U.S. elected official who served during or after 1956. Essays must have source citations. Applicants must register online before sending essays and have a nominating teacher review the essay. The winner and teacher will be invited to the Kennedy Library to accept the award, and the winner's teacher will

receive a grant. Essays are judged on content (55 percent) and presentation (45 percent).

Amount: $100-$20,000.

Number of Awards: Up to 25.

Deadline: January 4.

How to Apply: Applications are available online. A registration form and essay are required.

Leaders and Achievers Scholarship Program

Comcast Corporation
Comcast Center
1701 JFK Boulevard
Philadelphia, PA 19103
Phone: 855-670-4787
Email: comcast@applyists.com
http://corporate.comcast.com/our-values/community-investment/youth-education-leadership

Purpose: To provide one-time scholarship awards of $1,000 each to graduating high school seniors. Emphasis is on students who take leadership roles in school and community service and improvement.

Eligibility: Students must be high school seniors with a minimum 2.8 GPA, be nominated by their high school principal or guidance counselor and attend school in a Comcast community. See the website for a list of eligible communities by state. Comcast employees, their families or other Comcast affiliates are not eligible to apply.

Amount: $1,000.

Number of Awards: Varies.

Deadline: Varies.

How to Apply: Applications are available from the nominating principal or counselor.

Lending Tree $2,500 Scholarship

Lending Tree
11115 Rushmore Drive
Charlotte, NC 28277

Phone: 704-943-8714
https://www.lendingtree.com/about/scholarship

Purpose: To reward students who believe a college education is worth the money, time and effort.

Eligibility: Applicant must be a U.S. citizen who is a high school senior with a minimum 3.5 GPA. A short 30-second video response to the prompt found on the application is required. Applications are not judged on the quality of the video but on the actual response to the prompt.

Amount: $2,500.

Number of Awards: 1.

Deadline: July 15.

How to Apply: Applications are available online and must include a short video response, transcript, proof of citizenship, documentation of college acceptance and the name and address of the college that the student will attend.

Letters About Literature Contest

Letters About Literature
C. Gourley, Project Manager
81 Oliver Street
Wilkes-Barre, PA 18705
Phone: 202-707-5221
Email: cfbook@loc.gov
http://www.read.gov/letters/

Purpose: To encourage young people to read.

Eligibility: Applicants must be U.S. legal residents. They must be students in grades 4 through 12 and must be at least nine years old by the September 1 that precedes the contest deadline. They must submit a personal letter to an author about how that author's book or work has impacted them. Selection is based on letter originality, grammar and organization.

Amount: $200-$1,000.

Number of Awards: 6.

Deadline: December 2 and January 9.

How to Apply: Entry instructions are available online. An entry coupon and letter are required.

Lions International Peace Poster Contest

Lions Club International
300 W. 22nd Street
Oak Brook, IL 60523-8842
Phone: 630-571-5466
Fax: 630-571-1685
Email: pr@lionsclubs.org
http://www.lionsclubs.org
Purpose: To award creative youngsters cash prizes for outstanding poster designs.
Eligibility: Students must be 11, 12 or 13 years old as of the deadline and must be sponsored by their local Lions club. Entries will be judged at the local, district, multiple district and international levels. Posters will be evaluated on originality, artistic merit and expression of the assigned theme.
Amount: $500-$5,000.
Number of Awards: 24.
Deadline: November 15.
How to Apply: Applications are available from your local Lion's Club.

Live Mas Scholarship

Taco Bell Foundation
Email: info@livemasscholarship.com
http://www.livemasscholarship.com
Purpose: To support creators, innovators and dreamers in their pursuit of higher education.
Eligibility: Applicants must be between the ages of 16 and 24 and be U.S. citizens. Students will need to submit a short film of two minutes or less that shows or explains their life's passion. The film can be a short film, animation or simple personal testimonial. Selection is based on the ideas represented and not the expertise in creating a film.
Amount: $2,500-$25,000.
Number of Awards: 220.

Deadline: May 12.
How to Apply: Applications are available online.

Live Your Dream Awards Program

Soroptimist International of the Americas
1709 Spruce Street
Philadelphia, PA 19103
Phone: 215-893-9000
Fax: 215-893-5200
Email: siahq@soroptimist.org
http://www.soroptimist.org/awards/live-your-dream-awards.html
Purpose: To assist women entering or re-entering the workforce with educational and skills training support.
Eligibility: Applicants must be attending or been accepted by a vocational/skills training program or an undergraduate degree program. Applicants must be the women heads of household who provide the primary source of financial support for their families and demonstrate financial need. Applicants must submit their application to the appropriate regional office.
Amount: Up to $10,000.
Number of Awards: Varies.
Deadline: November 15.
How to Apply: Applications are available online.

LiveCareer

Email: scholarship@livecareer.com
http://www.livecareer.com/education-opportunities
Purpose: To support students with the cost of their education on the path to their career.
Eligibility: Applicants must write an attention-grabbing cover letter for their dream job at their dream company. Students must be currently enrolled full-time college or university students or scheduled to be enrolled full-time in a college or university for the semester

they would receive the scholarship. Applicants must be at least 18 years of age and should be legal residents of the United States.

Amount: $1,500.

Number of Awards: 3.

Deadline: April 3.

How to Apply: Applications are available online.

LULAC National Scholastic Achievement Awards

League of United Latin American Citizens
1133 19th Street NW
Suite 1000
Washington, DC 20036
Phone: 202-835-9646
Fax: 202-835-9685
Email: scholarships@lnesc.org
http://www.lnesc.org

Purpose: To aid students of all ethnic backgrounds attending colleges, universities and graduate schools.

Eligibility: Applicants do not need to be Hispanic or Latino to apply. Applicants must have applied to or be enrolled in a college, university or graduate school and be U.S. citizens or legal residents. Students must also have a minimum 3.5 GPA and if entering freshmen a minimum ACT score of 29 or minimum SAT score of 1350. Eligible candidates cannot be related to scholarship committee members, the Council President or contributors to the Council funds. Since applications must be sent from local LULAC Councils, students without LULAC Councils in their states are ineligible.

Amount: $2,000.

Number of Awards: Varies.

Deadline: March 31.

How to Apply: Applications are available online.

Make Me Laugh Scholarship

Unigo.com
220 NW 8th Avenue

Portland, OR 97209
Phone: 904-483-2930
https://www.unigo.com/scholarships/our-scholarships/

Purpose: To support students who wish to further their education.

Eligibility: Applicants must be at least 13 years old at time of application and must be legal residents of the United States. Students must be enrolled, or will be enrolled within six years at an accredited postsecondary institution. Applicants must describe a funny or embarrassing moment, fact or fiction, in 250 words or less.

Amount: $1,500.

Number of Awards: 1.

Deadline: November 30.

How to Apply: Applications are available online.

Marshall Memorial Fellowship

German Marshall Fund of the United States
1744 R Street NW
Washington, DC 20009
Phone: 202-683-2650
Fax: 202-265-1662
Email: info@gmfus.org
http://www.gmfus.org

Purpose: To provide fellowships for future community leaders to travel in Europe and to explore its societies, institutions and people.

Eligibility: Applicants must be nominated by a recognized leader in their communities or professional fields. They must be between 28 and 40 years of age and demonstrate achievement within their profession, civic involvement and leadership. They must be U.S. citizens or permanent residents or be permanent citizens of one of the 38 countries listed on the scholarship page. European applicants will visit the United States for their fellowship opportunities. Candidates should have little or no previous experience traveling through Europe. Fellows visit five or six cities and meet with policy makers, business professionals and other community leaders.

Amount: Varies.

Number of Awards: 75.

Deadline: September 28.

How to Apply: Applications are available online.

Mensa Education and Research Foundation Scholarship Program

Mensa Education and Research Foundation
1229 Corporate Drive West
Arlington, TX 76006
Phone: 817-607-5577
Fax: 817-649-5232
Email: info@mensafoundation.org
http://www.mensafoundation.org

Purpose: To support students seeking higher education.

Eligibility: Applicants do not need to be members of Mensa but must be residents of a participating American Mensa Local Group's area. They must be enrolled in a degree program at an accredited U.S. college or university in the academic year after application. They must write an essay explaining career, academic or vocational goals.

Amount: Varies.

Number of Awards: Varies.

Deadline: January 15.

How to Apply: Applications are available online in September. Please do NOT write to the organization to request an application. An application form and essay are required.

Most Valuable Student Scholarships

Elks National Foundation Headquarters
2750 North Lakeview Avenue
Chicago, IL 60614
Phone: 773-755-4732
Fax: 773-755-4733
Email: scholarship@elks.org

http://www.elks.org

Purpose: To support high school seniors who have demonstrated scholarship, leadership and financial need.

Eligibility: Applicants must be graduating high school seniors who are U.S. citizens and who plan to pursue a four-year degree on a full-time basis at a U.S. college or university. Male and female students compete separately.

Amount: $1,000-$12,500.

Number of Awards: 500.
Scholarship may be renewable.

Deadline: Varies.

How to Apply: Contact the scholarship chairman of your local Lodge or the Elks association of your state.

National College Match Program

QuestBridge
120 Hawthorne Avenue
Suite 103
Palo Alto, CA 94301
Phone: 888-275-2054
Fax: 650-653-2516
Email: questions@questbridge.org
http://www.questbridge.org

Purpose: To connect outstanding low-income high school seniors with admission and full four-year scholarships to some of the nation's most selective colleges.

Eligibility: Applicants must have demonstrated academic excellence in the face of economic obstacles. Students of all races and ethnicities are encouraged to apply. Many past award recipients have been among the first generation in their families to attend college.

Amount: Full tuition plus room and board.

Number of Awards: Varies.
Scholarship may be renewable.

Deadline: September.

How to Apply: Applications are available on the QuestBridge website in August of each year. An application form, two teacher recommendations, one counselor recommendation (Secondary School Report), a transcript and SAT and/or ACT score reports are required.

National D-Day Museum Online Essay Contest

National D-Day Museum Foundation
945 Magazine Street
New Orleans, LA 70130
Phone: 504-528-1944
Fax: 504-527-6088
Email: collin.makamson@ nationalww2museum.org
https://www.nationalww2museum.org/ students-teachers/school-programs
Purpose: To increase awareness of World War II by giving students the opportunity to compete in an essay contest.
Eligibility: Applicants must be high school or middle school students in the United States, its territories or its military bases. They must prepare an essay of up to 1,000 words based on a topic specified by the sponsor and related to World War II. Only the first 500 valid essays will be accepted.
Amount: Varies.
Number of Awards: Varies.
Deadline: December.
How to Apply: Applications are available online. An essay and contact information are required.

National Honor Society Scholarship

National Honor Society
c/o National Association of Secondary School Principals
1904 Association Drive
Reston, VA 20191
Phone: 703-860-0200
Fax: 703-476-5432
Email: nhs@nhs.us
https://www.nhs.us

Purpose: To recognize NHS members.
Eligibility: Applicants must be senior National Honor Society members. Applicants must demonstrate character, scholarship, service and leadership.
Amount: $2,325-$20,125.
Number of Awards: 400.
Deadline: February 6.
How to Apply: Application forms are available from your local NHS chapter adviser.

National Marbles Tournament Scholarship

National Marbles Tournament
Matt Corley
10908 Bornedale Drive
Hyattsville, MD 20783
Phone: 301-801-0795
Email: matt.corley@ nationalmarblestournament.org
https://www. nationalmarblestournament.org/
Purpose: To assist "mibsters," or marble shooters.
Eligibility: Applicants must win first place in a local marble tournament and then compete in the National Marbles Tournament held each summer in New Jersey. Students must be between 7 and 14 years old.
Amount: Varies.
Number of Awards: Varies.
Deadline: Varies.
How to Apply: Information on the tournament is available online.

National Merit Scholarship Program and National Achievement Scholarship Program

National Merit Scholarship Corporation
1560 Sherman Avenue, Suite 200
Evanston, IL 60201-4897
Phone: 847-866-5100
Fax: 847-866-5113
http://www.nationalmerit.org

Purpose: To provide scholarships through a merit-based academic competition.

Eligibility: Applicants must be enrolled full-time in high school, progressing normally toward completion and planning to enter college no later than the fall following completion of high school, be U.S. citizens or permanent legal residents in the process of becoming U.S. citizens and take the PSAT/NMSQT no later than the 11th grade. Participation in the program is based on performance on the exam.

Amount: $2,500.

Number of Awards: Varies.

Scholarship may be renewable.

Deadline: October PSAT test date.

How to Apply: Application is made by taking the PSAT/NMSQT test.

National Oratorical Contest

American Legion
Attn.: Americanism and Children and Youth Division
P.O. Box 1055
Indianapolis, IN 46206
Phone: 317-630-1249
Fax: 317-630-1369
Email: acy@legion.org
http://www.legion.org

Purpose: To reward students for their knowledge of government and oral presentation skills.

Eligibility: Applicants must be high school students under the age of 20 who are U.S. citizens or legal residents. Students first give an oration within their state and winners compete at the national level. The oration must be related to the Constitution of the United States focusing on the duties and obligations citizens have to the government. It must be in English and be between eight and ten minutes. There is also an assigned topic which is posted on the website, and it should be between three and five minutes.

Amount: $1,500-$18,000.

Number of Awards: Varies.

Deadline: Local American Legion department must select winners by March 18.

How to Apply: Applications are available from your local American Legion post or state headquarters. Deadlines for local competitions are set by the local Posts.

National Pathfinder Scholarship

National Federation of Republican Women
124 North Alfred Street
Alexandria, VA 22314
Phone: 703-548-9688
Fax: 703-548-9836
Email: mail@nfrw.org
http://www.nfrw.org

Purpose: To honor former First Lady Nancy Reagan.

Eligibility: Applicants must be female college sophomores, juniors, seniors or master's degree students. Two one-page essays and three letters of recommendation are required. Previous winners may not reapply.

Amount: $2,500.

Number of Awards: 3.

Deadline: June 1.

How to Apply: Applications are available online. An application form, three letters of recommendation, transcript, two essays and State Federation President Certification are required.

Newman Civic Fellow Awards

Campus Compact
45 Temple Place
Boston, MA 02111
Phone: 617-357-1881
Email: campus@compact.org
http://www.compact.org

Purpose: To provide scholarships and opportunities for civic mentoring to students with financial need.

Eligibility: Emphasis is on students who have demonstrated leadership abilities and significant interest in civic responsibility. Students must attend one of the 1,000 Campus Compact member institutions and be nominated by the Campus Compact member president. Applicants must be sophomores or juniors at four-year colleges or must attend a two-year college.

Amount: Varies.

Number of Awards: Varies.

Deadline: February.

How to Apply: Nominations must be made by the Campus Compact member president.

Off to College Scholarship Sweepstakes

SunTrust
P.O. Box 27172
Richmond, VA 23261-7172
Phone: 800-786-8787
http://www.suntrusteducation.com

Purpose: To assist a student for the first year of expenses at any accredited college.

Eligibility: Applicants must be high school seniors who are at least 13 years old and plan to attend a college accredited by the U.S. Department of Education the following fall. U.S. residency is required. Financial need and academic achievement are not considered. Note that this is a sweepstakes drawing every two weeks from October until mid-May.

Amount: Varies.

Number of Awards: Varies.

Deadline: May 12.

How to Apply: Applications are available online. Mail-in entries are also accepted. Contact information is required.

Optimist International Essay Contest

Optimist International
4494 Lindell Boulevard
St. Louis, MO 63108
Phone: 314-371-6000
Fax: 314-371-6006
Email: programs@optimist.org
http://www.optimist.org

Purpose: To reward students based on their essay-writing skills.

Eligibility: Applicants must be under 18 years of age as of December 31 of the current school year and application must be made through a local Optimist Club. The essay topic changes each year. Applicants compete at the club, district and international level. District winners receive a $2,500 scholarship. Scoring is based on organization, vocabulary and style, grammar and punctuation, neatness and adherence to the contest rules. The club-level contests are held in early February but vary by club. The deadline for clubs to submit their winning essay to the district competition is February 28.

Amount: $2,500.

Number of Awards: Varies.

Deadline: Early February.

How to Apply: Contact your local Optimist Club.

Patriot's Pen Youth Essay Contest

Veterans of Foreign Wars
406 W. 34th Street
Kansas City, MO 64111
Phone: 816-968-1117
Fax: 816-968-1149
Email: kharmer@vfw.org
https://www.vfw.org/community/youth-and-education

Purpose: To give students in grades 6 through 8 an opportunity to write essays that express their views on democracy.

Eligibility: Applicants must be enrolled as a 6th, 7th or 8th grader in a public, private or parochial school in the U.S., its territories or possessions. Home-schooled students and dependents of U.S. military or civilian personnel in overseas schools may also apply. Foreign exchange students and former applicants who placed in the national finals are ineligible. Students must submit essays based on an annual theme to their local VFW posts. If an essay is picked to advance, the entry is judged at the District (regional) level, then the Department (state) level and finally at the National level. Essays are judged 30 percent on knowledge of the theme, 35 percent on development of the theme and 35 percent on clarity.

Amount: Up to $5,000.

Number of Awards: 54.

Deadline: October 31.

How to Apply: Applications are available online or by contacting the local VFW office. Entries must be turned into the local VFW office. Contact information for these offices can be found online or by calling the VFW National Programs headquarters at 816-968-1117.

Power Poetry Scholarships

Power Poetry
295 East 8th Street
Suite 3W
New York, NY 10009
Phone: 347-460-6741
Email: help@powerpoetry.org
http://www.powerpoetry.org

Purpose: To reward students who write a slam poem.

Eligibility: Applicants must be 25 or younger and a U.S. citizen. Students submit their poem online.

Amount: $1,000.

Number of Awards: 1.

Deadline: Varies.

How to Apply: Applicants must join the website and submit their poem online.

Prompt's Scholarship

Prompt
110 E. 25th Street
New York, NY 10010
Phone: 844-577-6678
Email: scholarship@prompt.com

http://www.prompt.com/scholarship/

Purpose: To support students who are pursuing a higher education.

Eligibility: Applicants must be applying for admission at an accredited undergraduate institution within the U.S. or Canada for the following school year. Students will need to submit an essay as part of the application process. Finalists are selected one for each month of September, October, November and December with the grand prize given away in January. Applicants may enter a new essay each month.

Amount: $2,000-$10,000.

Number of Awards: 14.

Deadline: June 15.

How to Apply: Applications are available online.

Prudential Spirit of Community Awards

Prudential Financial Inc.
751 Broad Street, 16th Floor
Newark, NJ 07102
Phone: 973-802-4568
Fax: 973-802-4718
Email: spirit@prudential.com
https://spirit.prudential.com/awards/how-to-apply

Purpose: To recognize students for their self-initiated community service.

Eligibility: Applicants must be a student in grades 5-12 and a legal resident of one of the 50 states of the U.S. or District of Columbia and be engaged in a volunteer activity.

Amount: Varies.

Number of Awards: Varies.

Deadline: November 7.

How to Apply: Applications are available online.

Redfin Scholarship

Redfin
1099 Stewart Street
Suite 600

Seattle, WA 98101
https://www.redfin.com/resources/scholarship
Purpose: To support the pursuit of higher education.
Eligibility: Applicants must be U.S. residents. Students must have a minimum grade point average of 3.0 and be graduating high school seniors enrolling in an accredited post-secondary institution or current freshmen, sophomores or juniors at an accredited college or university.
Amount: $2,500.
Number of Awards: 2.
Deadline: July 31.
How to Apply: Applications are available online.

RentHop Apartment Scholarship

RentHop
101 Avenue of Americas
18th Floor
New York, NY 10013
Phone: 913-982-6682
Email: college-scholarship@renthrop.com
https://www.renthop.com/college_scholarship
Purpose: To support undergraduate students who display an entrepreneurial spirit as they pursue their college education.
Eligibility: Applicants must be a graduating high school senior or an undergraduate pursuing a bachelor's or an associate's degree. Students will need to submit a 500-word essay on the topic provided.
Amount: $1,000.
Number of Awards: 1.
Deadline: August 31.
How to Apply: An application consists of the essay being emailed to RentHop via a school email address. If applicant doesn't have a school email address, proof of enrollment will need to be provided.

Return 2 College Scholarship

R2C Scholarship Program
http://www.return2college.com/awardprogram.cfm
Purpose: To provide financial assistance for college and adult students with college or graduate school expenses.
Eligibility: Applicants must be college or adult students currently attending or planning to attend a two-year or four-year college or graduate school within the next 12 months. Students must be 17 years or older and U.S. citizens or permanent residents. The award may be used for full- or part-time study at either on-campus or online schools.
Amount: $1,000.
Number of Awards: Varies.
Deadline: January 31.
How to Apply: Applications are available online.

Rhodes Scholar

Rhodes Scholarship Trust
Attn.: Elliot F. Gerson
8229 Boone Boulevard, Suite 240
Vienna, VA 22182
Phone: 703-821-5960
Email: amsec@rhodesscholar.org
http://www.rhodesscholar.org
Purpose: To recognize qualities of young people who will contribute to the "world's fight."
Eligibility: Applicants must be U.S. citizens between the ages of 18 and 24 and have a bachelor's degree at the time of the award. The awards provides for two to three years of study at the University of Oxford including educational costs and other expenses. Selection is extremely competitive and is based on literary and scholastic achievements, athletic achievement and character.
Amount: Full tuition plus stipend.
Number of Awards: 32.
Deadline: October 4.

How to Apply: Applications are available online.

Ronald McDonald House Charities U.S. Scholarships

Ronald McDonald House Charities
1321 Murfreesboro Road
Suite 800
Nashville, TN 37217
Phone: 855-670-ISTS
Email: contactus@applyists.com
http://www.rmhc.org
Purpose: To help high school seniors attend college.
Eligibility: Applicants must be high school seniors less than 21 years of age who have a minimum 2.7 GPA. They must be U.S. residents who live in a participating Ronald McDonald House Charities chapter's geographic area. A list of chapters is on the website. There are four scholarships available: RMHC/Scholars, RMHC/Asia, RMHC/African-American Future Achievers and RMHC/HACER.
Amount: At least $1,000.
Number of Awards: Varies.
Deadline: January 20.
How to Apply: Applications are available online. An application form, transcript, personal statement, letter of recommendation and parents' tax forms are required.

Samuel Huntington Public Service Award

Samuel Huntington Fund
Attn: Amy Stacy
National Grid
40 Sylvan Road
Waltham, MA 02451
Phone: 508-389-2000
Email: amy.stacy@nationalgrid.com
https://www.nationalgridus.com
Purpose: To assist students who wish to perform one year of humanitarian service immediately upon graduation.

Eligibility: Applicants must be graduating college seniors, and must intend to perform one year of public service in the U.S. or abroad. The service may be individual work or through charitable, religious, educational, governmental or other public service organizations.
Amount: $15,000.
Number of Awards: Up to 3.
Deadline: January 17.
How to Apply: Applications are available online.

SanDisk Foundation Scholarship Program

c/o International Scholarship and Tuition Services Inc. (ISTS)
1321 Murfreesboro Road
Suite 800
Nashville, TN 37217
Phone: 855-670-ISTS
Email: contactus@applyists.com
http://www.sandisk.com/about-sandisk/corporate-responsibility/community/scholars-program/
Purpose: To assist students who have demonstrated leadership or entrepreneurial interests.
Eligibility: Applicants must be a high school senior or college freshman, sophomore or junior and must attend or plan to attend a full-time undergraduate program. Students must also demonstrate financial need. Up to 27 $2,500 renewable awards will given to students from the general public, up to three $2,500 renewable awards will be given to dependents of SanDisk employees and two students will be chosen as SanDisk Scholars and awarded full tuition scholarships for up to four years.
Amount: $2,500 to full tuition.
Number of Awards: Varies. Scholarship may be renewable.
Deadline: April 1.
How to Apply: Applications are available online. An application form and an essay are required.

Scholarship America Dream Award

One Scholarship Way
Saint Peter, MN 56082
Phone: 507-931-1682
Email: dreamaward@
scholarshipamerica.org
https://www.scholarsapply.org/
dreamaward
Purpose: To assist students in their second year or higher of post-secondary education.
Eligibility: Applicants must be U.S. citizens or permanent or legal residents who received a high school diploma from a U.S. school. Students must be planning to complete a minimum of one full year of post-secondary education and be planning to enroll as full-time undergraduates at the sophomore level or higher for the coming academic year. Applicants must have a grade point average of 3.0 or better.
Amount: $5,000-$15,000.
Number of Awards: Varies. Scholarship may be renewable.
Deadline: October 15.
How to Apply: Applications are available online.

Scholarships for Student Leaders

National Association for Campus Activities
13 Harbison Way
Columbia, SC 29212
Phone: 803-732-6222
Fax: 803-749-1047
Email: info@naca.org
https://www.naca.org/FOUNDATION/
Pages/Scholarships.aspx
Purpose: The NACA foundation is committed to developing professionals in the field of campus activities.
Eligibility: Applicants must be current undergraduate students who hold a significant campus leadership position, have made significant contributions to their campus communities and have demonstrated leadership skills and abilities.
Amount: Varies.
Number of Awards: Varies.
Deadline: December 31.
How to Apply: Applications are available online.

Scholastic Art and Writing Awards

557 Broadway
New York, NY 10012
Phone: 212-343-6100
Fax: 212-389-3939
Email: info@artandwriting.org
http://www.artandwriting.org/
scholarships/
Purpose: To reward creative young writers and artists.
Eligibility: Applicants must be in grades 7 through 12 in U.S. or Canadian schools and must submit writing pieces or portfolios in one of the following categories: dramatic script, general writing portfolio, humor, journalism, nonfiction portfolio, novel, personal essay/memoir, poetry, science fiction/fantasy, short story and short short story.
Amount: Up to $10,000.
Number of Awards: Varies.
Deadline: Varies.
How to Apply: Applications are available online.

Second Chance Scholarship Contest

American Fire Sprinkler Association
12750 Merit Drive
Suite 350
Dallas, TX 75251
Phone: 214-349-5965
Fax: 214-343-8898
Email: scholarship@firesprinkler.org
http://www.afsascholarship.org
Purpose: To help U.S. students pay for higher education.

Eligibility: Applicants must be U.S. citizens or legal residents and be high school graduates or GED recipients. They must be enrolled at an institution of higher learning no later than the spring semester of the upcoming academic year. American Fire Sprinkler Association (AFSA) staff and board member relatives are ineligible, as are past contest winners. Selection is made by random drawing from the pool of contest entrants.

Amount: $1,000.

Number of Awards: 5.

Deadline: August 30.

How to Apply: Contest entrants must read an informational article on fire sprinklers before taking a ten-question multiple choice test on the material covered in the article. The number of correct responses on the test is equal to the number of entries that will be made in the entrant's name, giving each entrant up to 10 entries to the random drawing that will determine the winners of the contest.

Siemens Competition in Math, Science and Technology

Siemens Foundation
170 Wood Avenue South
Iselin, NJ 08830
Phone: 877-822-5233
Fax: 732-603-5890
Email: foundation.us@siemens.com
http://www.siemens-foundation.org

Purpose: To provide high school students with an opportunity to meet other students interested in math, science and technology and to provide monetary assistance with college expenses.

Eligibility: Students must submit research reports either individually or in teams of two or three members. Individual applicants must be high school seniors. Team project applicants must be high school students but do not need to be seniors. Projects may be scientific research, technological inventions or mathematical theories.

Amount: $1,000-$100,000.

Number of Awards: Varies.

Deadline: September 20.

How to Apply: Applications are available online.

Simon Youth Foundation Community Scholarship

Simon Youth Foundation
225 W. Washington Street
Indianapolis, IN 46204
Phone: 800-509-3676
Fax: 317-263-2371
Email: syf@simon.com
http://www.syf.org/scholarships/

Purpose: To assist promising students who live in communities with Simon properties.

Eligibility: Applicants must be high school seniors who plan to attend an accredited two- or four-year college, university or technical/vocational school full-time. Scholarships are awarded without regard to race, color, creed, religion, gender, disability or national origin, and recipients are selected on the basis of financial need, academic record, potential to succeed, participation in school and community activities, honors, work experience, a statement of career and educational goals and an outside appraisal. Awards are given at every Simon mall in the U.S.

Amount: $1,500.

Number of Awards: Varies.

Deadline: Varies.

How to Apply: Applications are available online. Only the first 3,000 applications that the organization receives are considered.

Spirit of Anne Frank Awards

Anne Frank Center USA
44 Park Place
New York, NY 10007
Phone: 212-431-7993

Email: info@annefrank.com
http://annefrank.com/
Purpose: To reward students who lead the way in combating prejudice and injustice in their communities.
Eligibility: Students should be high school seniors, be U.S. citizens and plan on attending a four-year college or university in the fall of the upcoming academic year. Applicants must submit a 1,000-word essay characterizing their efforts and dedication toward achieving lasting change with regards to prejudice and intolerance.
Amount: $1,000-$10,000.
Number of Awards: Up to 5.
Deadline: February 19.
How to Apply: Applications are available online and must be submitted along with the essay and two letters of recommendation.

Stephen J. Brady STOP Hunger Scholarship

Sodexo Foundation
9801 Washingtonian Boulevard
Gaithersburg, MD 20878
Phone: 800-763-3946
Email: stophunger@sodexofoundation.org
http://www.sodexofoundation.org
Purpose: To aid students who have been active in the movement to eradicate hunger.
Eligibility: Applicants must be U.S. citizens or permanent residents. They must be students in kindergarten through graduate school who are enrolled at an accredited U.S. institution. They must have been active in at least one unpaid volunteer effort to end hunger during the past 12 months. Sodexo employees and previous recipients of this award are ineligible. Selection is based on the overall strength of the application.
Amount: $1,000-$5,000.
Number of Awards: Up to 25.
Deadline: December 5.

How to Apply: Applications are available online. An application form and supporting materials are required.

Stokes Educational Scholarship Program

National Security Agency (NSA)
Attn: MB3, Stokes Program
9800 Savage Road
Suite 6272
Ft. George G. Meade, MD 20755-6000
Phone: 410-854-4725
https://www.nsa.gov
Purpose: To recruit those with skills useful to the NSA, especially minority high school students.
Eligibility: Students must be seniors at the time of application, be U.S. citizens, have a 3.0 GPA, have a minimum ACT score of 25 or a minimum SAT score of 1200 and demonstrate leadership skills. Applicants must be planning to major in computer science or computer/electrical engineering.
Amount: Up to $30,000.
Number of Awards: Varies.
Scholarship may be renewable.
Deadline: October 31.
How to Apply: Applications are available online.

Stuck at Prom Scholarship

Henkel Consumer Adhesives
32150 Just Imagine Drive
Avon, OH 44011-1355
http://stuckatprom.com/
Purpose: To reward students for their creativity with duct tape.
Eligibility: Applicants must attend a high school prom as a couple in the spring wearing the most original attire that they make from duct tape. Both members of the couple do not have to attend the same school. Photographs of past winners are available on the website.
Amount: $1,000-$10,000.
Number of Awards: Varies.
Deadline: May 31.

How to Apply: Applications are available online. Contact information, release form and prom picture are required.

Student Transportation Video Contest

American Road and Transportation Builders Association
1219 28th Street, NW
Washington, DC 20007
Phone: 202-289-4434
Fax: 202-289-4435
Email: lshair@artba.org
http://www.artba.org

Purpose: To support students from elementary through graduate school interested in the transportation industry in the United States.

Eligibility: Applicants must be currently enrolled elementary through graduate school students. They must produce a 2-4 minute video on some aspect of the transportation industry in the United States. Selection is based on creativity and the overall strength of the video.

Amount: $500.

Number of Awards: 2.

Deadline: August 15.

How to Apply: Videos must be uploaded to You Tube and a link to the video sent to ARTBA by the submission deadline. Submission forms are available online. A submission form, waiver, link to the video, enrollment verification and photo release form are required.

Study Abroad Grants

Honor Society of Phi Kappa Phi
7576 Goodwood Boulevard
Baton Rouge, LA 70806
Phone: 800-804-9880
Fax: 225-388-4900
Email: awards@phikappaphi.org
http://www.phikappaphi.org

Purpose: To provide scholarships for undergraduate students who will study abroad.

Eligibility: Applicants do not have to be members of Phi Kappa Phi but must attend an institution with a Phi Kappa Phi chapter, have between 30 and 90 credit hours and have at least two semesters remaining at their home institution upon return. Students must have been accepted into a study abroad program that demonstrates their academic preparation, career choice and the welfare of others. They must have a GPA of 3.5 or higher.

Amount: $1,000.

Number of Awards: 75.

Deadline: February 15, September 15.

How to Apply: Applications are available online. An application form, personal statement, transcript, letter of acceptance and two letters of recommendation are required.

SuperCollege Scholarship

SuperCollege.com
Scholarship Dept. 673
2713 Newlands Avenue
Belmont, CA 94002
Email: supercollege@supercollege.com
http://www.supercollege.com/scholarship/

Purpose: SuperCollege donates a percentage of the proceeds from the sales of its books to award scholarships to high school, college, graduate and adult students.

Eligibility: Applicants must be high school students, college undergraduates, graduate students or adult students residing in the U.S. and attending or planning to attend any accredited college or university within the next 12 months. The scholarship may be used to pay for tuition, books, room and board, computers or any education-related expenses.

Amount: $1,000.

Number of Awards: 1.

Deadline: October 31.

How to Apply: Applications are available online.

Technology Addiction Awareness Scholarship

Digital Responsibility
3561 Homestead Road #113
Santa Clara, CA 95051-5161
Email: scholarship@
digitalresponsibility.org
http://www.digitalresponsibility.org
Purpose: To help students understand the negative effects of too much screen time.
Eligibility: Applicant must be a high school, college, graduate or home schooled student who is a U.S. citizen or legal resident. A 140-character message about technology addiction is required to apply. The top 10 applications will be selected as finalists; finalists will be asked to write a full length 500- to 1,000-word essay about technology addiction. Only online applications are accepted.
Amount: $1,000.
Number of Awards: 1.
Deadline: January 30.
How to Apply: Applications are available online.

Telluride Association Summer Programs

Telluride Association
217 West Avenue
Ithaca, NY 14850
Phone: 607-273-5011
Fax: 607-272-2667
Email: tasp-queries@
tellurideassociation.org
http://www.tellurideassociation.org
Purpose: Summer program to provide high school students with a college-level, intellectually enriching experience.
Eligibility: Applicants must be high school juniors. The association seeks applicants from a variety of socio-

economic backgrounds and provides for their tuition and room and board during summer programs in New York and Michigan. Students are invited to apply either by receiving a score on the PSAT/NMSQT that is usually in the top 1 percent or by nomination by a teacher or counselor.
Amount: Summer program tuition and fees.
Number of Awards: Varies.
Deadline: January 24.
How to Apply: Applications are sent to nominated students.

The Akash Kuruvilla Memorial Scholarship

Akash Kuruvilla Memorial Scholarship Fund Inc.
P.O. Box 140900
Gainesville, FL 32614
Email: akmsfinfo@gmail.com
https://www.akmscholarship.com
Purpose: To continue the legacy of Akash Jacob Kuruvilla.
Eligibility: Applicants must be entering or current full-time college students at an accredited U.S. four-year college or university. They must demonstrate academic achievement, leadership, integrity and excellence in diversity. Selection is based on character, financial need and the applicant's potential to impact his or her community.
Amount: $1,000.
Number of Awards: 2.
Deadline: June 30.
How to Apply: Applications are available online. An application form, essay, personal statement, one recommendation letter and resume are required.

Truman Scholar

Truman Scholarship Foundation
712 Jackson Place NW
Washington, DC 20006
Phone: 202-395-4831

Fax: 202-395-6995
Email: office@truman.gov
http://www.truman.gov
Purpose: To provide college junior leaders who plan to pursue careers in government, non-profits, education or other public service with financial support for graduate study and leadership training.
Eligibility: Applicants must be juniors, attending an accredited U.S. college or university and be nominated by the institution. Students may not apply directly. Applicants must be U.S. citizens or U.S. nationals, complete an application and write a policy recommendation.
Amount: Up to $30,000.
Number of Awards: 55-65.
Deadline: February 7.
How to Apply: See your school's Truman Faculty Representative or contact the foundation.

U.S. Bank Scholarship Program

U.S. Bank
c/o U.S. Bank Office of Corporate Citizenship
1420 Kettner Boulevard
7th Floor
San Diego, CA 92101
Phone: 800-242-1200
http://www.usbank.com/community/financial-education/scholarship.html
Purpose: To support graduating high school seniors who plan to attend college.
Eligibility: Applicants must be high school seniors who plan to attend or current college freshmen, sophomores or juniors attending full-time at an accredited two- or four-year college and be U.S. citizens or permanent residents. Recipients are selected through a random drawing.
Amount: $20,000.
Number of Awards: Varies.
Deadline: October 27.

How to Apply: Applications are only available online.

U.S. JCI Senate Scholarship Grants

U.S. JCI Senate
106 Wedgewood Drive
Carrollton, GA 30117
Email: tom@smipc.net
http://www.usjcisenate.org
Purpose: To support high school students who wish to further their education.
Eligibility: Applicants must be high school seniors and U.S. citizens who are graduating from a U.S. accredited high school or state approved home school or GED program. Winners must attend college full-time to receive funds. Applications are judged at the state level.
Amount: $1,000.
Number of Awards: Varies.
Deadline: January 15.
How to Apply: Applications are available from your school's guidance office.

U.S. News Path to College Scholarship Program

Scholarship America
One Scholarship Way
Saint Peter, MN 56082
Phone: 507-931-1682
Email: usnews@scholarshipamerica.org
https://www.scholarsapply.org/usnews
Purpose: To support students who plan on entering college upon graduation from high school.
Eligibility: Applicants must be attending a U.S. public or private high school and plan to enroll full-time at an accredited four-year college or university in the U.S. immediately following graduation. A minimum GPA of a 3.0 is required. Applicants must be U.S. citizens.
Amount: $2,500.

Number of Awards: 2.
Deadline: June 2.
How to Apply: Applications are available online.

Voice of Democracy Audio Essay Contests

Veterans of Foreign Wars
406 W. 34th Street
Kansas City, MO 64111
Phone: 816-968-1117
Fax: 816-968-1149
Email: kharmer@vfw.org
https://www.vfw.org/community/youth-and-education
Purpose: To encourage patriotism with students creating audio essays expressing their opinion on a patriotic theme.
Eligibility: Applicants must submit a three- to five-minute audio essay on tape or CD focused on a yearly theme. Students must be in the 9th to 12th grade in a public, private or parochial high school, home study program or overseas U.S. military school. Foreign exchange students are not eligible for the contest, and students who are age 20 or older also may not enter. Previous first place winners on the state level are ineligible.
Amount: $1,000-$30,000.
Number of Awards: Varies.
Deadline: October 31.
How to Apply: Applications are available online but must be submitted to a local VFW post.

Wendy's High School Heisman Award

Wendy's Restaurants
One Dave Thomas Boulevard
Dublin, OH 43017
Phone: 800-205-6367
Email: jdeets@scholarshipamerican.org
http://www.wendysheisman.com
Purpose: To recognize high school students who excel in academics,

athletics and student leadership.
Eligibility: Applicants must be entering their high school senior year and participate in one of 43 officially sanctioned sports. Eligible students have a minimum 3.0 GPA. Selection is based on academic achievement, community service and athletic accomplishments.
Amount: $1,000-$10,000.
Number of Awards: 100.
Deadline: October 3.
How to Apply: Application forms are available online.

Young Patriots Essay Contest

National Center for Policy Analysis
14180 Dallas Parkway
Suite 350
Dallas, TX 75254
Phone: 972-308-6487
Email: rachel.stevens@ncpa.org
http://www.ncpa.org/youth
Purpose: To assist high school students who write about public policy.
Eligibility: Applicants must write an essay up to 1,200 words on the public policy topic provided. Students must be current high school students or recent high school graduates who have never enrolled in any college or university excluding AP or dual credit classes taken during high school.
Amount: $2,000-$5,000.
Number of Awards: 3.
Deadline: January 1.
How to Apply: Application information is available online.

Young People for Fellowship

People For the American Way Foundation
Young People For
1101 15th Street NW
Suite 600
Washington, DC 20005
Phone: 202-467-4999
Email: mhall@pfaw.org
http://www.youngpeoplefor.org

Purpose: To encourage and cultivate young progressive leaders.

Eligibility: Applicants must be undergraduate students and be interested in promoting social change on their campuses and in their communities. Selection is based on the overall strength of the application.

Amount: Varies.

Number of Awards: Varies.

Deadline: December 31.

How to Apply: Applications are available online. An application form is required.

Young Scholars Program

Jack Kent Cooke Foundation Young Scholars Program
301 ACT Drive
P.O. Box 4030
Iowa City, IA 52243
Phone: 800-941-3300
Fax: 703-723-8030
Email: scholarships@jkcf.org
http://www.jkcf.org

Purpose: To help high-achieving students with financial need and provide them with educational opportunities throughout high school.

Eligibility: Applicants must have financial need, be in the 7th grade and plan to attend high school in the United States. Academic achievement and intelligence are important, and students must display strong academic records, academic awards and honors and submit a strong letter of recommendation. A GPA of 3.65 is usually required, but exceptions are made for students with unique talents or learning differences. The award is also based on students' will to succeed, leadership and public service, critical thinking ability and participation in the arts and humanities. During two summers, recipients must participate in a Young Scholars Week and Young Scholars Reunion in Washington, DC.

Amount: Varies.

Number of Awards: 60.
Scholarship may be renewable.

Deadline: April 5.

How to Apply: Applications are available online and at regional talent centers. An application form, parental release, financial and tax forms, school report, teacher recommendation, personal recommendation and survey form are required.

ZipRecruiter $3,000 Scholarship Challenge

ZipRecruiter
1453 3rd Street Promenade #335
11th Floor
Santa Monica, CA 90401
Phone: 404-936-1644
https://www.ziprecruiter.com/scholarship

Purpose: To promote the use of creativity in the career search.

Eligibility: Applicants must be college students at least 18 years of age who are legal residents of the United States or its territories and possessions. Students are to write an essay on the topic provided. A minimum 2.5 GPA is required.

Amount: $3,000.

Number of Awards: 1.

Deadline: September 30.

How to Apply: Applications are available online.

About the Authors

Harvard graduates Gen and Kelly Tanabe are the founders of SuperCollege and the award-winning authors of 14 books including *The Ultimate Scholarship Book, Get Free Cash for College, The Ultimate Guide to America's Best Colleges, Get into Any College* and *Accepted! 50 Successful College Admission Essays.*

Together, Gen and Kelly were accepted to every school to which they applied and all of the Ivy League colleges, and won over $100,000 in merit-based scholarships. They were able to leave Harvard debt-free and their parents guilt-free.

Gen and Kelly give workshops at high schools across the country and write the nationally syndicated "Ask the SuperCollege.com Experts" column. They have made dozens of appearances on television and radio and have served as expert sources for respected publications including *U.S. News & World Report, USA Today, The New York Times,* the *New York Daily News,* the *Chronicle of Higher Education, Money, Woman's Day* and *CosmoGIRL.*

Gen grew up in Waialua, Hawaii, and was the first student from Waialua High School to attend Harvard. He graduated magna cum laude from Harvard with a degree in both History and East Asian Studies.

Kelly attended Whitney High School, a nationally ranked public high school in her hometown of Cerritos, California. She graduated magna cum laude from Harvard with a degree in Sociology.

Gen, Kelly and their sons Zane and Kane live in Belmont, California.